TOPICAL MEMORY SYSTEM
LIFE ISSUES

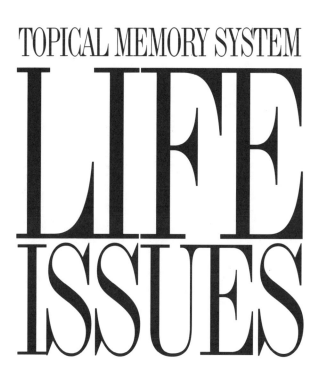

NAVPRESS
A MINISTRY OF THE NAVIGATORS
P.O.BOX 35001, COLORADO SPRINGS, COLORADO 80935

Contents

INTRODUCTION
What's Scripture Memory and Meditation All About?

Here's the situation: You *know* that God's Word is great spiritual food, that you need to get *His* perspective on your crazy, hectic life. And yet you also know that you're not quite sure where to look in the Bible for words of wisdom on your overwhelming personal problems. Furthermore, you know very well that you're just not good at memorizing. And besides, you're so totally maxed out that you can't even find a free minute to sit down to a small, nourishing bowl of that spiritual food.

Well, this Scripture memory package is designed to make the whole process so easy—and even fun—that you won't have to shift gears at all. You can start by putting a verse card on your bathroom mirror to help you think about what God's trying to communicate to you. That's right! While you're brushing your teeth! You can meditate further about that Scripture passage while you're stuck in a traffic jam on your way to work. Then you can read the brief chapter on that topic while you're taking your lunch break. And you can ponder the three "Questions for Meditation" while you're stuck in the traffic jam on the way back from work. How's that for a plan?!

If you're able to find a little extra time to dig in further, there are additional Scripture references at the end of each chapter. But the important thing is to not allow the thought of Scripture memory and meditation to overwhelm you. We all memorize grocery lists, telephone numbers, people's names, street addresses, and so on. You'll find that getting a grasp on Bible verses is just as doable.

But why bother?
God is trying to communicate with us. We may not have a clue about what He is trying to say, but when God talks, we need to pay attention. Well, Scripture is one of God's primary ways of getting through to us. His *Word* has been rendered in *words*, preserved for us in the pages of the Bible. What better place could we go in order to know His mind and His will?

The most substantial way to solve your deepest problems is to take them to God in prayer, *and* to find His solutions in Scripture. In prayer, we call out to the living God from the depths of our soul; in Scripture memory and meditation, we find that God is calling to us from the depths of His living Word.

You can really count on God's help as you meditate and memorize. He will guide you through the life-changing process of internalizing His profound truth. First, God will give you a real hunger for His deep wisdom and counsel in Scripture. Second, He will help you digest His Word as you meditate upon it and memorize it. Finally, as you learn to focus on Scripture in a very personal way, taking God's Word to heart, He will encourage you to put that truth into action in your life.

Both memory and meditation are vitally important. Scripture memory puts God's Word in your mind. Prayerful meditation puts God's Word in your heart. Having the mind of God directing your life can really help you overcome your anxieties. You can experience God's transforming peace by knowing His promises and having them written deep inside of you.

God wants to speak to you through His Word so that you can face the incredible spiritual battle that is looming in your life every single day. God tells us, "Keep my words and store up my commands within you. . . . Write them on the tablet of your heart" (Proverbs 7:1,3). When God's Word is established in your heart, you have a big sword to use when you fight against all the dark forces that are mounted against you (Ephesians 6:10-18). Using that powerful sword will help keep you spiritually fit, and you'll be far better equipped to meet future needs and opportunities.

Why take the time to memorize and meditate on Scripture? Because failing to do so could be harmful to your spiritual health. God calls us to embrace His Word—not as a suggestion but as a command (Deuteronomy 6:6-7, Proverbs 7:1-3, Colossians 3:16).

Why these topics?

All of us deal with challenges in our everyday lives that are difficult for us to handle. If we want to know what God has to say about these problem areas, we need to immerse our mind and soul in His Word, which has been spoken to *us*. There is a certain power in Scripture that can jar us out of our complacency, comfort us in our times of darkest sorrow, and guide us through the complex labyrinth of life on this fallen planet. Scripture represents God's calling to us, His attempt to get our attention.

The twelve topic areas covered in the *Topical Memory System: Life Issues* are common struggles we face in this complex, uncertain world—what we often call "the real world." As you meditate on Bible passages that relate to your most pressing questions and concerns, and then memorize those passages, you will find that God will guide you and help you grow in ways that you could not have anticipated.

But as you confront the holy perspective of God in His Word, you will find that you need to blast away your personal illusions and begin to expand your vision. Only then can you discover what is truly the *real* world, in contrast to the unreal world of sin and suffering and despair.

As you memorize and meditate on verses from a particular topic, remember that God wants to enter this area of your life in a way that will meaningfully change your whole way of thinking and living. As Paul said, "Do not conform any longer to the pattern of this world, but be transformed by the renewing of your mind. Then you will be able to test and approve what God's will is—his good, pleasing and perfect will" (Romans 12:2).

Remember the references

Knowing the reference (chapter and verses) for each passage you memorize makes it possible to find it in the Bible quickly when you need it for personal use or in helping others. So make the reference a part of each passage you memorize.

The surest way to remember the reference is to say it both before *and* after the passage each time you review it. This will connect the reference and the passage in your mind.

When learning or reviewing a passage, you may want to make it a habit to say the topic first, then the reference, then the Scripture passage itself, and the reference again at the end. This may seem tedious at first, but it can be extremely effective in reinforcing the passage in your memory.

The verse cards

Topic ——— **Knowing God's Will**   NIV ——— Version

Romans 12:2

Passage ——— Do not conform any longer to the pattern of this world, but be transformed by the renewing of your mind. Then you will be able to test and approve what God's will is—his good, pleasing and perfect will.   ——— Reference

Romans 12:2

When is the best time to memorize?

Memorizing Scripture is easier when you can concentrate without distraction. Two of the best times are just before you go to bed at night, and early in the morning, perhaps in conjunction with your devotional time. A few minutes at lunchtime or just before supper may also work well for you.

Use spare moments during the day—while you are waiting or walking, for example—to review your verses. You might consider developing the habit of carrying your verse pack with you.

How much should you memorize?

Certain people have a greater capacity, interest, and opportunity to memorize Scripture. But everyone can memorize. After all, we have no problems memorizing the names, times, and channels of our favorite television programs. You may want to start out with one memory card per week. But eventually you may be ready to adjust upward. It is more important to have a few verses clearly memorized than to have a slew of fuzzy recollections.

Why learn it "word-perfect"?

Make it a constant goal to quote a passage perfectly, word-for-word. It's actually easier to learn verses correctly from the start. This also makes it easier to review them later. Knowing them word-for-word will also give you greater confidence in using your verses in your everyday life.

Once you have chosen a particular Bible translation for the verses you memorize, it may be better to learn all your verses in that translation, rather than mixing in others, which could be potentially confusing.

HOW TO MEDITATE ON SCRIPTURE

Meditation is not mind-wandering or mind-emptying. It has a form and an object. Meditation is directing our thoughts to a single topic. It is thinking with a purpose, asking God to direct our thoughts.

Biblical meditation doesn't have to be a solemn, academic exercise. It requires an attitude of curiosity and expectation, and leads to exciting discoveries, a refreshed spirit, and transformation of character. It is a crucial step toward fully knowing and obeying God's will.

Here are five methods of meditation you may want to try:

1. *Paraphrasing.* You could gain some exciting insights when you rewrite a Scripture passage in your own words. This exercise can be one where you use an expanded paraphrase with as many words as necessary to express the full meaning, or you might enjoy the challenge of using as few words as possible.

Here's an example of the kind of expanded paraphrase you could write. Isaiah 26:3 reads, "You will keep in perfect peace him whose mind is steadfast, because he trusts in you." You could paraphrase this, "You will give personal well-being, a lasting kind of harmony, freedom from anxiety, a *shalom* kind of peace, to the person who trusts You completely, without any doubts in his mind."

2. *Asking questions.* You can sort through the information in a passage by asking *who, what, where, why,* and *how* questions, or by jotting down random questions that come to mind as you memorize and reflect on that

passage. (You may not come up with answers for all your questions.)

For Isaiah 26:3 you could ask, *"Who* does God give perfect peace to?" *"What* attitude toward God do I need to have in my mind?" and *"Why* does God provide this perfect peace?"

3. *Praying.* Pray over the passage. Praise God for the way His character is revealed in the verse; thank Him for any promises you see, and you may want to ask Him to apply these in your own life; and confess any failure that the passage may bring to mind.

"Think out loud" with God as you meditate.

4. *Emphasizing different words or phrases.* This simple exercise involves fixing your focus on small parts of the passage and how they relate to the passage as a whole.

For Isaiah 26:3, you could emphasize the following words and think of their implications: "You will *keep* in perfect peace," "You will keep in *perfect* peace," "You will keep in perfect *peace*," and so on.

5. *Finding cross-references.* Try to think of other passages that relate directly to the meaning of the passage you are memorizing. Looking for the relationships between various parts of Scripture can be stimulating, and will help you gain an overall view of the major themes in God's Word.

Again considering Isaiah 26:3, you might think of Philippians 4:6-7, 1 Peter 5:7, or Matthew 11:28.

In all these forms of meditation, relate the passage to your own circumstances. Suppose you are worried and restless and are not experiencing inner peace. You know this doesn't please God, but you feel that you can't help it. You decide to meditate on Isaiah 26:3 as a source of help.

As you think about this verse, you ask yourself, "What does it mean to have perfect peace? Is this really available to me? How can I trust God more?"

Then you might make a list of the things that trouble you. For each item on your list you ask, "Am I ready to trust God to take care of these things for me? Am I willing to make a conscious effort to really trust Him?"

Some Christians confuse Bible knowledge with spiritual maturity, assuming that knowing more about the Bible automatically makes them better Christians. This is just not true. Many of the Pharisees knew the Old Testament, yet they were spiritual phonies. *The key to spiritual maturity is applying God's Word to your life.*

HOW TO MEMORIZE SCRIPTURE

You'll want to refer to these principles often in the coming weeks:

As you start to memorize a passage—

1. Read the article in this book that corresponds with each topic in order to give you an overview of that life issue.

2. Read in your Bible the surrounding context of each passage you memorize.

3. Try to gain a clear understanding of what each passage actually means. (You may want to check other translations or paraphrases to get a better grasp of the meaning.)

4. Read the passage through several times thoughtfully, either aloud or in a whisper. This will help you grasp the passage as a whole. Each time you read it, you should say the topic, reference, passage, and then the reference again.

5. Discuss the passage with God in prayer, and continue to seek His help for success in Scripture memory.

While you are memorizing the passage—

6. Work on saying the passage aloud as much as possible.

7. Learn the topic and reference first.

8. After learning the topic and reference, learn the first phrase of the passage. Once you have learned the topic, reference, and first phrase, and you have repeated them several times, continue adding more phrases after you can quote correctly what you have already learned.

9. Think about how the passage applies to you and your daily circumstances. The more meaningful a passage is to you, the easier it is to remember.

10. Always include the topic and reference as part of the passage as you learn and review it.

After you can quote correctly the topic,
reference, passage, and reference again—

11. It is helpful to write the passage out from memory, then check on yourself to see if you have written it correctly. This deepens the impression in your mind.

12. Review the passage immediately after learning it, and repeat it frequently in the next few days. This is a crucial step for getting the passage firmly fixed in mind, because of how quickly we tend to forget something recently learned.

13. After you have memorized all six passages for a certain topic, read and ponder the "Questions for Meditation" in the chapter on that topic. Write down several major things you have learned about that life issue, and also list some practical things you could (and should) do in your own life to apply what you have learned. Simply meditating on Scripture and memorizing it are not enough. It's important to God that we also obey and apply His Word in our own lives. That's how God's Word comes alive!

14. Review! Review! Review! Repetition is probably the best way to engrave the verses permanently on your memory. Review on your own, and

also with someone else. Ask that other person to hold your cards while you recite the verses word-for-word. When you hesitate, you want that other person to give you only a minor cue when you're not sure of the next phrase.

15. Go on to the "Additional Scripture References" if you want to memorize and meditate on more passages in a particular topic. There are some extra verse cards that are blank. You can fill in passages that are especially meaningful to you, and then slide each card into the verse card holder and take it with you as you move about during the day.

SUCCESSFUL SCRIPTURE MEMORY

Don't get discouraged if your Scripture memory work begins to seem too routine. The process of recording Scripture on your mind and heart does have a somewhat mechanical aspect. It requires certain methods and a great deal of perseverance. But as long as the process of imprinting God's Word on your heart is moving forward, these Scriptures will be continually available to help you with life issues.

There are certain helpful things you can do if your Scripture memory program begins to seem lifeless. Try spending more time going over your Scripture passages in prayer and meditation. Also begin using the passages in your conversations or in letters. New freshness can come as you share the Scriptures with others.

Keep in mind that memorizing and meditating on these Scriptures is a practical way of making them available to God to use in your life.

Now on to the real spiritual food!

1
KNOWING GOD'S WILL

What Does God Want From Me?
Warren and Ruth Myers

God is good. He wills only the best for us.

Though He is great and awesome, owning and sustaining every star and galaxy in our immense universe, He cares about us as persons. He has designed us with rich capacities for enjoyment—for tasting, seeing, feeling, thinking, loving, achieving, and worshiping—and He "richly supplies us with all things to enjoy" (1 Timothy 6:17, NASB).

The One who designed the complexities of space and the intricacies of the atom, who is all-wise and all-knowing, has in mind a plan for each of our lives. His plan perfectly complements and develops the unique personality He envisioned before He made the world. God's plan dovetails precisely with the calling and contribution He has in mind for each of us. The person and the plan were conceived together in His heart, tailor-made for each other.

God's plan is realistic. It takes into account the mistakes and failures He knew would occur—and even our sins, which grieve Him deeply. But He never says, "Oops! What should I do now?!" His plan includes the ways He will weave our wrong decisions and actions into the best possible outcome for us and for others, as well as for His greatest glory.

In the Bible, through commands and principles, God has revealed His general will for all of us. Beyond this, His specific will for each of us includes the personal guidance He offers and the circumstances He permits or causes to happen. Over and over the Bible reminds us that fitting in with His will, both general and personal, assures our well-being and the highest fulfillment of our potential, now and forever.

Mentally we may agree that God's plan is for our greatest good. But often our struggles and reactions show that we don't truly believe it. We may feel we know better than God what is good for us. To some of us, "good" means being ourselves whether we are right or wrong. It means getting what we think we want, when we want it—a present sense of pleasure, relief, or achievement.

God also cares about our present joy, but even more He wants to ripen our capacity for enjoyment in every aspect of our person. He wants us to learn a stable happiness that is not threatened by what happens to us. He wants us to go beyond the dribbles of satisfaction we try to force out of life.

We are losers whenever we decide to do our own thing instead of God's will. Any happiness we are able to squeeze from life by going our own way is soon marred by inner conflict. The honey gets mixed with sand. The peace we feel evaporates like dew under a scorching sun, giving way to inner disturbance or depression. The dividends we accumulate range from what is second best to what is mediocre or even intolerable.

God's plan liberates us from the emotions that rob us of joy, such as hostility toward others, or the distress of feeling we never quite measure up, or the fear of what people think of us, or anxiety about our ability to cope with life. His plan brings true love into our lives—His limitless, unconditional love flowing in to meet our needs and flowing out to meet the needs of others.

Into this He blends peace, gladness, and the sense of fulfillment that comes from making a significant contribution in life.

So when God asks us to yield to Him and His plan, His goal is not to limit us or deprive us of a satisfying, exciting life. When He asks us to surrender our personal plans or preferences, He offers us something better. Surrendering to Him always makes us become more than we could ever envision or achieve ourselves.

God does not destroy personality—He enhances it. He delivers us from the inner imprisonment of our imagined independence. He does this at a cost—the surrender of our autonomy. It is a cost well worth paying.

This can be our prayer: "Father, use Your work to make me feel deeply Your love and goodness and wisdom. Correct my false ideas about You that make me shrink back from Your plan for me. Give me a long-range view that believes You for the best in life today, through all the weeks and years ahead, and forever. Work in me a glad surrender of all that I am and all that I have."

We found the following fable in *Song Offerings* by Rabindranath Tagore, an Indian educator and poet who believed in one God. Again and again, Tagore's simple, vivid story motivates us to give ourselves wholly to our true and living God.

> I had gone a-begging from door to door in the village path, when thy golden chariot appeared in the distance like a gorgeous dream, and I wondered who was this King of all kings!
>
> My hopes rose high and I thought my evil days were at an end, and I stood waiting for alms to be given unasked and for wealth scattered on all sides in the dust.
>
> The chariot stopped where I stood. Thy glance fell on me and

thou camest down with a smile. I felt that the luck of my life had come at last. Then of a sudden thou didst hold out thy right hand and say, "What hast thou to give to me?"

Ah, what a kingly jest was it to open thy palm to a beggar to beg! I was confused and stood undecided, and then from my wallet I slowly took out the least little grain of corn and gave it to thee.

But how great my surprise when at the day's end I emptied my bag on the floor to find a least little gram of gold among the poor heap. I bitterly wept, and wished that I had had the heart to give thee my all!

MAJOR PRINCIPLES—A CHECKLIST

In making your decisions on a daily basis, ask God to give you wisdom step by step, hour by hour. Trust the Holy Spirit to work through your mind and your knowledge of God's Word, guiding your thinking and sanctifying your common sense. When it comes to the tougher major decisions, the principles in the following checklist can help you discover God's "good, pleasing and perfect will" (Romans 12:2).

For some years we have been using this checklist with great profit. In major decisions such as getting engaged and going overseas as missionaries, we have gone over it in detail. Sometimes for several months we have kept a running record of light the Holy Spirit has given us through these principles, then prayerfully reviewed the list as the time of decision approached.

We find that often the Lord doesn't use all the principles in guiding us. Sometimes He gives us one or two big thousand-watt lights. At other times He gives many small fifty-watt ones that make us equally sure of His leading. If we come to amber lights or red lights, we evaluate further, and usually wait for clarification.

Here are the principles:

The big three

1. *Lordship*—Am I willing to do God's will, whatever it may be? This is the indispensable foundation for finding His will.

> "If anyone would come after me, he must deny himself and take up his cross daily and follow me." (Luke 9:23)

> Offer your bodies as living sacrifices. (Romans 12:1)

2. *God's Word*—What principles, commands, or prohibitions from the

15

Scriptures apply to this decision? Has God given me any promises or motivating verses on the subject?

> The unfolding of your words gives light. (Psalm 119:130)

3. *Prayer*—Do I have continued inner peace as I consider these principles in prayer? As I pray about a specific possibility, do I have continued freedom in prayer, or lack of it? Prayer also includes asking God for the inner working of the Holy Spirit, who is the Spirit of wisdom, understanding, and counsel.

> Do not be anxious about anything, but in everything, by prayer
> and petition, with thanksgiving, present your requests to God.
> (Philippians 4:6)

Others

4. *My God-given priorities, gifts, and calling*—What gifts and abilities has God given me, and how does He want me to use these to accomplish His purposes in the world? What course of action is most in line with the long-range inclinations He has built into me?

> I consider my life worth nothing to me, if only I may finish the race
> and complete the task the Lord Jesus has given me—the task of testifying to the gospel of God's grace. (Acts 20:24)

> There are different kinds of gifts . . . different kinds of service . . .
> different kinds of working. (1 Corinthians 12:4-6)

5. *The continued inner promptings of the Holy Spirit*—Does He motivate me either toward or away from a particular course of action?

> Teach me to do your will, for you are my God; may your good Spirit
> lead me on level ground. (Psalm 143:10)

> They tried to enter Bithynia, but the Spirit of Jesus would not allow
> them to. (Acts 16:7)

6. *Godly counsel*—What is the prayerful counsel of someone who knows me and is somewhat familiar with the situation? Am I avoiding or disregarding counsel that I should consider?

Listen to advice and accept instruction, and in the end you will be wise. (Proverbs 19:20)

Plans fail for lack of counsel, but with many advisers they succeed. (Proverbs 15:22)

7. *Providential circumstances*—Has God arranged events to point clearly in one direction? If I am facing obstacles, are they God's way of stopping me? Or are they Satanic hindrances to be overcome by faith?

In all things God works for the good of those who love him. (Romans 8:28)

What he opens no one can shut, and what he shuts no one can open. (Revelation 3:7)

8. *Practical information*—What research can I do to uncover facts that might influence my decision, such as reading, consulting with knowledgeable people, writing letters of inquiry, or taking an exploratory trip?

The heart of the discerning acquires knowledge; the ears of the wise seek it out. (Proverbs 18:15)

9. *Personal insights and preferences*—What does my common sense tell me? Do I have any special insights? What are my feelings and desires, as well as the feelings and desires of those who will be affected by this decision? Which of these factors seem to be from God? Which seem to be temptations to make a wrong, a self-indulgent, or a second-best choice?

Delight yourself in the LORD and he will give you the desires of your heart. (Psalm 37:4)

Do not love the world or anything in the world. (1 John 2:15)

10. *Peace*—Do I have continued inner peace as I consider these principles in prayer? Or do I experience restlessness, impatience, or inner conflict?

If our hearts do not condemn us, we have confidence before God. (1 John 3:21)

11. *Timing*—What is God's mind about the *when* of this decision? Are my emotions pressing me to move too fast? Or am I holding back too long

before stepping out—perhaps through fear, or by waiting too long for conclusive evidence?

> Wait for the LORD; be strong and take heart and wait for the LORD. (Psalm 27:14)

> Now finish the work, so that your eager willingness to do it may be matched by your completion of it, according to your means. (2 Corinthians 8:11)

12. *Faith*—Does God want me to step out by faith—trusting Him to take care of the consequences to myself and others, and to overrule if I make a sincere mistake?

> Commit your way to the LORD. (Psalm 37:5)

> Trust in the LORD with all your heart and lean not on your own understanding. (Proverbs 3:5)

To use this list effectively, we suggest that you write down the thoughts the Lord gives you as you consider the principles. Arrange your ideas under three column headings: "Pros" (positive factors and advantages), "Cons" (negative factors and disadvantages), and "Other Considerations" (alternatives, neutral factors).

In emotionally loaded issues, try to give greater weight to the more objective principles. Don't rely only on peace, for example, or only on personal desires and feelings.

SEEKING GUIDANCE THROUGH THE SCRIPTURES
In seeking guidance from God's Word, we should give primary attention to the commands and principles for living that apply to all believers. Occasionally God guides us (or confirms guidance already given) by impressing us with a special verse that seems exactly suited to our situation. This is a valid form of guidance. But we must be careful to recognize the subjective element in it, avoiding the possible dangers of relying on it too much, and refraining from being dogmatic about our conclusions. We should ask ourselves:

Is this God speaking, or am I merely finding confirmation for what I want? (It is possible to make the Scriptures say things we want to hear, and to ignore passages that teach something different.)

Do other avenues of finding God's will (such as my own willingness to obey, scriptural principles, continued prayer, and godly counsel) confirm my impressions, or do they cast doubt on their accuracy?

Do I approach the Bible by looking for verses to leap out at me, and so miss the overall teachings of Scripture and personal fellowship with the living God?

Am I seeking an easy method of finding God's will, a "Christian" substitute for horoscopes and Ouija boards, instead of carefully determining what God wants and then making mature decisions?

Sometimes people find promises and interpret them as specific assurances about the future. Then, when things do not turn out as they expect, they become disillusioned, perhaps even doubting the Bible's trustworthiness. They fail to realize that they have simply misinterpreted what God said and misclaimed the promises.

This need not be humiliating or discouraging. Our mistakes can remind us not to force the Bible into saying what we want to hear. They can spur us to approach the Scriptures with the primary purpose of knowing God better, and learning to see things as He does so that we can walk in His ways.

> Happy are we to have God's Word always to guide us! What is the mariner without his compass? And what is the Christian without the Bible? This is the unerring chart, the map in which every shoal is described, and all the channels from the quicksands of destruction to the haven of salvation mapped and marked by One who knows all the way.
>
> —*C. H. Spurgeon*

SUPERNATURAL GUIDANCE

God can, and sometimes does, guide us in miraculous or spectacular ways—such as Peter's vision in Acts 10. But these are exceptional occurrences, and not the usual way God leads us.

Elisabeth Elliot, in *A Slow and Certain Light*, made the following observations about guidance by miraculous means:

> But there is one thing we ought to notice about these miracles. When God guided by means of the pillar of cloud and fire, by the star of Bethlehem, by visitations of angels, by the word coming through visions and dreams and prophets and even through an insulted donkey, in most cases these were not signs that had been asked for. And when they were asked for, as in the case of Jehoshaphat and Ahab, they were not accepted.
>
> Supernatural phenomena were given at the discretion of the divine wisdom. It is not for us to ask that God will guide us in some miraculous way. If, in his wisdom, he knows that such means are what we need, he will surely give them.

If God chooses a spectacular method to guide us, we surely will not miss it! But if we constantly seek spectacular or dramatic guidance (including direct verbal revelations), we may miss the enrichment and maturity that come as we daily tune in to His Word, His Spirit, and His other usual ways of showing us His will.

Warren and Ruth Myers, Navigator missionaries in southern Asia, are authors of Discovering God's Will, *published by Warren and Ruth Myers, The Navigators, 117 Lorong K, Telok Kurau, Singapore 1542.*

QUESTIONS FOR MEDITATION

1. If you could ask God any question at all about His will for your life, what would it be? Go ahead and ask Him.
2. Do you think God has a "Plan A" and a "Plan B," a specific set of instructions, for every event in your life? Does He care whether you buy a Ford or a Chevrolet? Exactly what is His most important concern, His "will," for your life (see Romans 12:2)?
3. Think of some times when your will clashed with God's will. What can you learn from those experiences?

VERSE CARD REFERENCES

Proverbs 16:9, Proverbs 3:5-7, Jeremiah 29:11-13, Romans 12:2, Isaiah 30:21, 1 John 5:14-15

ADDITIONAL SCRIPTURE REFERENCES

Gen. 50:19-20; **Ex.** 18:15-16; **Lev.** 24:10-12; **2 Sam.** 7:20-21; **1 Chron.** 13:1-2; **Ezra** 10:10-11; **Job** 37:5; **Ps.** 19:13; 25:12; 27:14; 37:4; 40:8; 51:12; 119:130; 143:10; **Prov.** 3:5-7; 9:10; 11:2; 12:15; 15:22; 16:1,9,25; 18:15; 19:3,20-21; 20:24; **Eccl.** 3:1-12; 7:14; 8:6-7,16-17; 11:5; **Is.** 1:18-20; 26:12; 28:21; 30:21; 41:4; 43:18-19; 53:10-11; 55:8-9; **Jer.** 10:23; 29:11-13; **Lam.** 3:26; **Dan.** 4:35; **Mic.** 6:8; **Mt.** 6:9-10; 7:21; 10:29-30; 12:50; 18:14; 23:37-38; 26:39-41; **Lk.** 9:23; 12:47-48; **Jn.** 1:12-13; 4:34; 6:28-29,38-40; 7:17; 9:31; **Acts** 4:27-29; 16:7; 18:20-21; 20:24-27; 22:14-15; **Rom.** 8:14, 20-21,28; 9:11-24; 11:33-36; 12:1-3; **1 Cor.** 12:4-6; **2 Cor.** 8:11; **Eph.** 1:9-11; 5:8-17; 6:5-8; **Phil.** 1:9-11; 2:12-13; 4:6; **Col.** 1:9; 3:15; 4:12; **1 Thes.** 4:3-8; 5:18; **Heb.** 2:4; 5:14; 10:5-10, 35-36; 13:20-21; **James** 1:5-8; 4:13-17; **1 Pet.** 2:15-16; 3:17; 4:1-2,19; **1 Jn.** 2:15-17; 3:21; 5:14-15; **Rev.** 3:7.

2
SELF-IMAGE
When Your Mirror Needs Adjusting
Ralph Ennis

Can you look in a mirror and honestly love the person you see there? Can you explain to someone else who you really are and how much you are worth? If you can, you are apparently in the minority.

Some estimates indicate that 90 percent of Americans lack a healthy self-image. James Dobson, in *What Wives Wish Their Husbands Knew About Women*, cites lack of self-esteem as the number one problem among wives he surveyed.

THREE IMPORTANT CONCEPTS
In seeking a solution, we need to thoroughly examine self-image, self-worth, and self-love.

Self-image is your view of yourself. In Romans 12:3 we are admonished to have a proper self-image: "Do not think of yourself more highly than you ought, but rather think of yourself with sober judgment, in accordance with the measure of faith God has given you." Do not be either haughty or self-debasing in your estimation of yourself. Know yourself accurately.

Self-worth is the value you place on yourself. Perhaps you place proper value on yourself, treating yourself and others with love, or possibly you despairingly abuse yourself after giving up hope of possessing any value. The goal should be to believe and understand your God-given value.

Self-love is your love of yourself. Jesus said, "Love your neighbor as yourself" (Luke 10:27). Loving yourself is thus quite biblical. Self-love is not arrogance and should not be disdained. We should learn to love ourselves.

These three concepts have an interdependent relationship with one another. Your view of yourself—your self-image—influences the value you place on yourself; and the value you place on yourself directly contributes to the degree that you love yourself.

How should we view ourselves? How should we value ourselves? The answers to these questions are prerequisites to learning to love ourselves.

HOW SHOULD WE VIEW OURSELVES?

Each of us must assimilate two aspects of our nature into our self-image.

The first of these is our *being*, or our *intrinsic* nature. God has created all of us with many uniform characteristics of being. In Genesis 1:27 we see that "God created man in his own image . . . male and female he created them." We are not God, but we are made in His image. God is a person, and is eternal. We too are persons, and have eternal destinies.

Our intrinsic nature also includes a reflection of God's moral character. He is a God of love, truth, holiness, and justice. Though blemished by sin, we still partially manifest the moral image of God. We can, in His likeness, manifest love, understand and communicate truth, distinguish holiness, and strive for justice.

The second aspect of our nature we must consider is our *doing*, or our *functional* nature. God said, "Be fruitful and increase in number; fill the earth and subdue it. Rule over the fish of the sea and the birds of the air and over every living creature that moves on the ground" (Genesis 1:28).

He also commanded, "Go and make disciples of all nations, baptizing them in the name of the Father and of the Son and of the Holy Spirit, and teaching them to obey everything I have commanded you" (Matthew 28:19-20).

God had given each of us diverse abilities in order that we may obey these commands to be fruitful, increase, fill, subdue, rule, and make disciples. Each individual is created differently. Through years of experience and through God's gracious leading, we distinguish our abilities and develop them in a fashion that glorifies Him.

We must accept our limited abilities. God is all-knowing; we know just a little. He is all-powerful; we have little power. He is present everywhere; our presence is limited by time and space. He is sovereign; we have only the authority that He gives us. He created things out of nothing; we create expressions of our personalities, intellect, feelings, and imaginations out of a limited framework—ourselves and the world in which we live. God can meet all needs—spiritual, emotional, mental, physical; though naturally talented and spiritually gifted, we can meet only a limited scope of needs.

Every person has a wonderful and yet sin-blemished nature of *being* and *doing*. This nature can be regenerated by the Holy Spirit as we believe in Christ, for "if anyone is in Christ, he is a new creation; the old has gone, the new has come!" (2 Corinthians 5:17). We are wonderfully made and wonderfully *re-created* in Christ.

We should enjoy and express our God-given nature. In Psalm 139:14, David says, "I praise you because I am fearfully and wonderfully made; your works are wonderful, I know that full well."

God wants *us* to know "full well" this kind of wonderful sense of how He made us!

HOW SHOULD WE VALUE OURSELVES?

How should we value our being (our intrinsic nature) and our doing (our functional nature)?

Our materialistic culture values a person for his actions rather than his being. An engineer is worth $50,000 a year for his work. A student is worthy of honor if he makes straight A's. A woman is esteemed more highly if she has risen to an executive job. Good professional athletes are paid six-figure or seven-figure salaries and idealized as heroes.

We often value lightly, however, the garbage collector, the "D" student, the housewife, and many others.

Let's add two terms to our discussion—*intrinsic worth* and *functional worth*. Intrinsic worth is a measure of a person's worth for what he *is*—his being, his inborn and reborn intrinsic nature. Functional worth is a measure of a person's worth for what he *does*—his functions, his actions.

To illustrate these concepts, let's consider two people. John is thirty-five. He is a researcher for a major chemical firm and is financially secure. He is happily married and has two wonderful children. As a church elder, he ministers extensively. He is a success by most standards.

Linda is also thirty-five. But she is physically deformed, her arms and legs misshapen and nonfunctional. She is also blind, deaf, and mute. Her intellectual ability is far below average. Her parents, who are divorced, never visit her. She is often sick for months. Until she dies, Linda will remain in a hospital as an unloved financial burden on society.

What is John's functional worth as compared with Linda's? John has great functional worth to his society, his family, his church, and himself, while Linda has little to contribute in those areas. If John bases his love for himself on what he does, then he has good reason to love himself. Linda, however, will detest herself if she evaluates only her performance.

But John and Linda are more than their actions. They share the *same* intrinsic nature and value to God. Let's explore why.

God values each individual as a person created in His image.

"Look at the birds of the air; they do not sow or reap or store away in barns, and yet your heavenly Father feeds them. Are you not much more valuable than they?" (Matthew 6:26)

"How much more valuable is a man than a sheep!" (Matthew 12:12)

The day of the Lord will come like a thief. The heavens will disappear with a roar; the elements will be destroyed by fire, and the earth and everything in it will be laid bare. Since everything will be destroyed in this way, what kind of people ought you to be? You ought to live holy and godly lives as you look forward to the day of

God and speed its coming. That day will bring about the destruction of the heavens by fire, and the elements will melt in the heat. But in keeping with his promise we are looking forward to a new heaven and a new earth, the home of righteousness. (2 Peter 3:10-13)

These three passages teach us that God values us more than birds, more than sheep, and more than the present physical universe—which He will destroy, but out of which He will preserve His children eternally.

So then, to what are we equal in value? Paul said, "You were bought at a price" (1 Corinthians 6:20). That price is our value to God. And that magnificent and sacrificial payment was the death of God's Son, Jesus Christ. God did not sacrifice His chief angel for us, or even all of His angels. He did not relinquish real estate or spend gold. To demonstrate His love for us, He gave His beloved Son to pay the price to redeem mankind. This is our great value. We can have none greater.

But do we deserve it? No, not on our own merit. After sin entered into the world we became worthless, fit only to be destroyed. "All have turned away, they have together become worthless; there is no one who does good, not even one" (Romans 3:12). Nevertheless, God, in His mercy and love, has assigned great value to us through Christ! "God demonstrates his own love for us in this: While we were still sinners, Christ died for us" (Romans 5:8).

We should thus have a lofty evaluation of our worth—and yet many of us do not.

MANY OF US DISLIKE OURSELVES

Remember the words of Isaiah:

> "Woe to him who quarrels with his Maker, to him who is but a
> potsherd among the potsherds on the ground. Does the clay say to
> the potter, 'What are you making?' Does your work say, 'He has no
> hands?' Woe to him who says to his father, 'What have you begot-
> ten?' or to his mother, 'What have you brought to birth?' " (45:9-10)

Nevertheless, many of us do dislike ourselves. We may dislike our physical appearance or intellectual limits, or our background and lack of opportunities. Or we may loathe our personality. How has this occurred?

As our self-image and self-worth are undermined, our self-love either deteriorates or never develops. Since our society often teaches that we can say nothing absolute about our worth, and that man came into being only by chance, exists as only a speck, and can be obliterated in an instant, it should come as no surprise that so many people have a contorted sense of self-love.

24

Other factors also enter in. We may value ourselves for our function in society rather than for our intrinsic nature. Yet we find that ideas of functional worth are unequal and varied. A doctor or business executive may be highly valued, but manual laborers or farmers tend to receive little esteem. On another level, a fetus may be deemed worthless and may be aborted as an unwanted inconvenience, while another baby is born and brings joy into a couple's life.

Why are people valued so differently? Is it wrong to be a farmer or a manual laborer? Absolutely not. But it is wrong to compare ourselves with others. Paul said, "We do not dare to classify or compare ourselves with some who commend themselves. When they measure themselves by themselves and compare themselves with themselves, they are not wise" (2 Corinthians 10:12).

Not all comparing is harmful. A doctor must compare his degree of proficiency with that of his colleagues so he will know when to refer a case to another physician. Such comparisons are necessary in evaluating our competency in certain areas.

However, a problem of distorted self-worth arises when we compare our functions (our doings or actions) with those of others in order to establish our worth. Such comparisons usually lead us to one of two conclusions: We either feel superior or inferior to the other person. But either conclusion is wrong. All of us have equal intrinsic value.

The two distortions of self-worth—feelings of prideful superiority or debasing inferiority—may manifest themselves in numerous symptoms. We may relate to authority improperly. Some people act in a rebellious manner to draw attention to themselves or to prove themselves. Others oversubmit and become people pleasers in order to be esteemed by others. All of these are wrong.

Some people seek attention through manipulation, going around pretending to be sick, mad, happy, or concerned. These self-gratifying techniques may serve to satisfy our wishes to attract the attention of others to ourselves, but their effects are only temporary.

Certain people seek a perverse kind of self-worth through unbiblical sexual relations. Still others have mannerisms such as loud laughing or constant joking, which they have found effective in getting attention.

It is common to see people in leadership positions lead others improperly. Authoritarian leaders often put others down in order to build themselves up. The overprotective leader shields his followers for fear that their failure will make him lose face. Or a leader may abdicate his responsibilities, wishing simply to preserve a past record.

Still another symptom of distorted self-worth is an unhealthy view of our capacity to achieve. Some people would never consider trying a new sport, a new language, a new job, or a new adventure, simply because they fear failure and the anticipated subsequent loss of face. Others are characterized by overconfident ambition. Never admitting limitations, they pridefully press on, sometimes to the detriment of themselves or others.

The inferior-feeling, insecure person may quickly recognize his self-debasing symptoms. The superior-feeling, overconfident person, however, does not often see his problem as quickly. Pride covers his eyes. He is over-confident in the area of self-love, though his self-love is distorted and ill-founded. God often has to use hard and humbling circumstances to convince this person of his need for a proper self-image, self-worth, and self-love.

These symptoms often result from a legitimate desire for self-worth, though other root problems—ignorance, willful rebellion, and bondage to sin—can also lead to signs of a poor self-concept. But nothing can free us from these feelings as long as we persist in comparing ourselves with others. We need to recognize that we need not compare. We are not superior or inferior in value. None of us can have higher value than others. Christ died for all.

LEARNING TO LOVE OURSELVES

There is hope for those of us who mildly dislike or even intensely hate ourselves. We can all learn to love ourselves. God has given five biblical steps to guide us in this pursuit.

First, we need to ask God to forgive our sin of self-degradation or shameful haughtiness stemming from comparison. God has promised us forgiveness (1 John 1:9). We need to be forgiven. This is our necessary starting point.

Second, we must rely on the Holy Spirit to produce change. Spiritual growth does not come through human effort, but is the result of God's power working in us. We rely on Him by praying that He will enable us to properly view, value, and love ourselves. And we must learn to trust that He will answer our prayer—perhaps not the way we hope, but He will answer.

Third, God commands us to renew our minds. In Romans 12:2, Paul said, "Do not conform any longer to the pattern of this world, but be trans-formed by the renewing of your mind. Then you will be able to test and approve what God's will is—his good, pleasing and perfect will." The world values a man for what he does. God values men for who they are. We must not be conformed to the world's thinking, but rather be transformed to the mind-set of God.

This can be done by replacing our erroneous thoughts about ourselves with God's thoughts about us. We need to study, memorize, and meditate on such passages as Genesis 1–3, Psalm 139, Ezekiel 16, John 3:16, and Ephesians 1–3. Then we will learn who we are as creatures in God's image, sinners in Adam's image, and saints being transformed into Christ's image.

Our minds must be renewed by believing that God values us and loves us as He values and loves His Son! We must not disdain anything that God loves, including ourselves.

Fourth, our comparisons must cease—now! Since our worth is based on the price God paid for us, we cannot increase our value through comparing. Since we do not need to compare, we are free to stop. Practically speaking, when you recognize that you are comparing yourself with others, immediately stop and pray. Thank God for the way He has made you and values you despite what you perceive to be your shortcomings.

And fifth, we need to be patient. A distorted self-image does not occur quickly, and will probably not leave quickly. An improper pattern of evaluating yourself may have begun in early childhood, and the habit of comparing yourself with others may seem rather innate by now. So we must persevere in following these biblical steps.

BALANCING SELF-LOVE AND SELF-DENIAL

Self-love is not a guise for self-indulgence. Jesus calls us not only to love ourselves but also to deny ourselves. Jesus loved Himself, for God *is* love—and yet, "being found in appearance as a man, he humbled himself and became obedient to death—even death on a cross!" (Philippians 2:8).

Self-love is loving oneself in humility before God. It is not self-indulgence or serving oneself. Rather, self-love gives us a basis by which we can sacrificially love and serve others with humility. If we love ourselves, we have no legitimate need to compare ourselves with others, to covet others, to put others down, or to compete with others for glory.

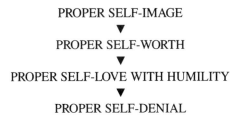

PROPER SELF-IMAGE
▼
PROPER SELF-WORTH
▼
PROPER SELF-LOVE WITH HUMILITY
▼
PROPER SELF-DENIAL

A proper self-worth is believing that God values you and has bought you at an incalculable price to Himself—the death of His Son.

A true self-love reflects an understanding and acceptance of God's perspective of your image and value, and of His love for you. This kind of love is humble toward self, but caring and serving toward others. It is not arrogant or self-indulgent.

An accurate self-image is seeing yourself as God sees you—as a creature, a sinner, and a saint.

Ralph Ennis is a Navigator representative in Raleigh, North Carolina.

QUESTIONS FOR MEDITATION

1. The mythological character Narcissus fell in love with his own image. In what ways are you infatuated with your own image? Take some time to reevaluate that inflated opinion of yourself.
2. When we reflect on who we really are—our appearance and our character—we can also become overly critical. In what ways have you been too hard on yourself?
3. God is shaping us to be "conformed to the likeness of his Son" (Romans 8:29). In what areas do you see that kind of growth in your life? How can being like Him set you free to truly be yourself?

VERSE CARD REFERENCES

Psalm 139:13-14a, 1 Samuel 16:7b, Jeremiah 9:23-24a, Philippians 2:3-5, 1 Peter 3:3-4, Matthew 10:29-31

ADDITIONAL SCRIPTURE REFERENCES

Gen. 1:26-28; **1 Sam.** 16:7; **Ps.** 8:3-6; 139:13-14; **Prov.** 3:5-7; 26:12; 27:2,19; 28:26; **Eccl.** 7:29; **Is.** 45:9-10; **Jer.** 9:23-24; 17:5; **Mt.** 6:26; 7:12; 10:29-32; 12:12; 18:3-4; 28:19-20; **Mk.** 8:34-36; 9:35; **Lk.** 9:23,25; 12:15; **Jn.** 3:16; **Acts** 10:15; **Rom.** 8:28-31; 9:20-21; 12:2-3; **1 Cor.** 1:18-31; 6:19-20; 15:10; **2 Cor.** 3:4-6,18; 5:17; 10:12-13,17-18; **Gal.** 1:10; 2:20; 6:3-5; **Eph.** 2:10; **Phil.** 2:3-11,21; 3:7-9; **James** 1:22-25; **1 Pet.** 3:3-4; **2 Pet.** 3:10-13; **1 Jn.** 1:9; **Rev.** 3:17.

3
DEALING WITH SIN
Confronting the Shadow Within
Jerry Bridges

When Irwin Moon, founder of the Moody Institute of Science, was leaving home to start his own career, his godly father gave him a Scripture verse as his parting counsel. "Remember, Irwin," he said, " 'If we confess our sins, he is faithful and just and will forgive us our sins and purify us from all unrighteousness' " (1 John 1:9).

That father's parting counsel to his son probably strikes most of us as a bit strange. We'd try to think of some great promise from the Bible to give our son or daughter. But is there any greater promise in all the Bible than 1 John 1:9? What Christian doesn't need every day both the reminder of the need for confession and the assurance that, upon confession, God does forgive us and cleanse us from all unrighteousness?

Yet 1 John 1:9, as needful and precious as it is, is probably one of the most abused verses in all the Bible. We abuse it in two ways: first, by an almost flippant use of it when we regard our sin too lightly, and second, by a sense of despair that we have sinned so often or so grievously that we have exhausted God's forgiveness. These two abuses are at opposite extremes, but both result from a failure to view our sin as God views it.

On the one hand, we fail to see the seriousness of our sin, and on the other hand, we fail to see the completeness of God's forgiveness.

To help us get the most value from the great promise of 1 John 1:9, let us consider God's view of sin.

THE SERIOUSNESS OF SIN

To see sin as God sees it, we must first consider the seriousness of all sin. For too long we have tended to categorize sin into the part that is unacceptable and the part that can be tolerated. We have reached a state of peaceful coexistence with sins of the thought life, sins where "nobody gets hurt," and little habits or personality traits that are dismissed as "that's just the way I am."

But God takes a serious view of sin. Three passages of Scripture in the Old Testament will help us to see how seriously God views our sin.

29

The first passage is Leviticus 16:21. In describing the ritual of the scapegoat, the goat that would bear all the sins of the children of Israel away into the desert, the Lord, speaking through Moses, said:

> "He [the priest] is to lay both hands on the head of the live goat and confess over it all the wickedness and rebellion of the Israelites—all their sins—and put them on the goat's head."

In this verse God calls the sins of the Israelites *wickedness* and *rebellion*. Perhaps you've never thought of your own sins—gossip, resentment, covetousness, and perhaps lustful thoughts—as rebellion, but that is how God views them.

In most English versions of the Bible the word *transgression* is used to translate the Hebrew word that the NIV translates as rebellion. It literally means a rejection of God's authority. That is why it is considered rebellion. Sin in any form, be it ever so small or insignificant in our sight, is rebellion against the authority of a sovereign God.

As the supreme Lawgiver, God has the authority to tell us how to live, and He has done this in His Word. As the psalmist said, "You have laid down precepts that are to be fully obeyed" (Psalm 119:4). God has not only given us precepts; He expects us to obey them diligently and completely.

Let's consider just one example: Over and over again the Bible tells us to guard our tongues, to speak only words that are both truthful and helpful to our hearers. Are we diligent about obeying these instructions? If not, we are rebelling against the authority of a sovereign God. We may feel we are just being careless, that we are perhaps not quite as diligent as we should be—but God says it is rebellion. Our hasty, unkind, and critical words are not just carelessness; they are acts of defiance.

Our pastor sometimes uses the expression, "shaking our fists in God's face." At first I was a little startled by that expression. I never felt that I was shaking my fist in God's face. But that is what our sins are—acts of rebellion indicating a fist in the face of God.

The second passage that will help us see how God views sin is 2 Samuel 12:9-10. After David had committed adultery with Bathsheba and had had her husband Uriah killed, God sent the prophet Nathan to rebuke David. In the midst of his stinging rebuke to David, God said through Nathan, "Why did you despise the word of the LORD by doing what is evil in his eyes? You struck down Uriah the Hittite with the sword and took his wife to be your own. You killed him with the sword of the Ammonites. Now, therefore, the sword will never depart from your house, because you despised me and took the wife of Uriah the Hittite to be your own."

David in his sinful acts *despised* both the Word of God and the Person of God. You may think, "Well, that's only right. David's adultery and conspiracy to murder were totally reprehensible. He did despise God." But what did Jesus say? In the Sermon on the Mount He said hateful thoughts are murder and a lustful look is adultery (Matthew 5:21-22,27-28). Most of us who are familiar at all with the teachings of Scripture know very well what Jesus taught about hate and lust, yet we sometimes indulge such thoughts anyway. We are not committed to total obedience. But to the extent that we are not committed to total obedience, we show that we despise God and His Word.

The third passage that shows us God's view of sin is 1 Kings 13:21. God sent a prophet to testify against the idolatrous altar that King Jeroboam had built in Samaria. As God commissioned this prophet, He commanded him, "You must not eat bread or drink water [in Samaria] or return by the way you came" (verse 9). But in the process of returning to Judah, the man of God was deceived by an old prophet, and *did* stop to eat and drink in Samaria. As he was eating, the word of God came to the old prophet and he said, "This is what the LORD says: 'You have defied the word of the LORD and have not kept the command the LORD your God gave you.'"

God accused the prophet of *defying* His Word. Now admittedly this is a difficult passage. It appears the man of God intended to fully obey God (in fact, he turned down an invitation to dine at the king's table), but was deceived by the older prophet. Yet God calls his action a defiance of His Word, and because of that defiance, the man of God lost his life.

God's judgment seems rather severe to us. After all, as the saying goes, "Nobody got hurt." Yet that is just the point. Sin is not to be judged on the basis of whether anybody gets hurt, but on the basis that it is disobedience—a *defiance*, according to God—to God's sovereign law. As W. S. Plummer said in *Psalms*, "We never see sin aright until we see it as against God. . . . All sin is against God in this sense: that it is His law that is broken, His authority that is despised, His government that is set at naught."

If we want to avoid the first abuse of 1 John 1:9—regarding our sin too lightly and claiming God's forgiveness too casually, perhaps even presumptuously—we must begin to view sin as God views it. We need to see it as rebellion against His authority, as despising His Person, and as defiance of His law.

If you have been guilty of treating 1 John 1:9 too casually (and who of us hasn't?), try substituting *rebellion* or *defiance* or *despising God's Word* for the word *sin* as you plead that verse before God. "Lord, I confess my rebellion and despising of Your Word and I plead Your promise of forgiveness and cleansing." As we do this, we will begin to view our sin as God views it and will be less likely to abuse the gracious promise of God by treating it too casually.

31

THE FORGIVENESS OF GOD

Oftentimes, however, we err in the other direction by limiting the forgiveness promised by God. Perhaps we have committed some grievous sin—at least to our own minds. Or, more likely, we have fallen for the thousandth time before some temptation that easily entangles us. At such times we are prone to think that we have exhausted the limits of God's forgiveness. We feel that God's gracious promise of forgiveness in 1 John 1:9 just doesn't apply anymore. The sin is too big or the occurrences too frequent. And so, instead of experiencing the gracious forgiveness and cleansing of God, we are weighed down by our own sense of guilt.

To avoid this error, we need to see God's view of our sin as it is forgiven in Christ. Several Old Testament passages use different figures of speech to point out the extent of God's forgiveness of our sins. The first is Psalm 103:12: "As far as the east is from the west, so far has he removed our transgressions from us."

One Sunday our pastor pointed out to us that you can start north at any place on the earth, and if you continued in that direction, you would eventually be going south. But that is not true when you go east or west. If you start west and continue in that direction, you will always be going west. North and south meet at the North Pole and South Pole, but east and west never meet.

So how far is the east from the west? Well, they never meet or even come close to meeting. They are an infinite distance apart. And God has said He removes our transgressions (our rebellious acts) an infinite distance from us.

God uses another figurative expression in Isaiah 38:17. There the prophet says, "In your love you kept me from the pit of destruction; you have put all my sins behind your back." When something is behind our back, we can't see it. God, through the prophet Isaiah, says that He has done that with our sins. He has put them behind His back so that He cannot see them anymore. Our sins are not just behind God's back. He has *put* them there and He has done this deliberately. He does not want to see our sins anymore.

The third picturesque expression God uses to show the completeness of His forgiveness occurs in Micah 7:19. There the prophet Micah says of God, "You will tread our sins underfoot and hurl all our iniquities into the depths of the sea." Years ago as a naval officer, I had some personal experience with the depths of the sea. In a boating accident our ship lost some valuable equipment. Because we were operating in fairly shallow water (around 100 feet deep), we spent all of the following day "fishing" for that equipment with grappling hooks. We never recovered any of it. It was buried in the depths of the sea.

That is the way God views our sins. They didn't just "fall overboard" into the sea; God Himself *hurled* them into the depths where they could never be recovered, never be seen again, or brought to His mind.

A fourth passage that emphasizes the completeness of God's forgiveness is Isaiah 43:25: "I, even I, am he who blots out your transgressions, for my own sake, and remembers your sins no more." Here God uses two expressions. He *blots out* our transgressions—that is, He removes them from the record—and He *remembers them no more*. God's ability to forget is much better than ours. Long after we have forgiven someone, we can call back to mind that offense and, if we are not careful, begin to hold it against that person once more. But God's forgiveness is complete and permanent. He not only blots our acts of rebellion and defiance off the official record; He also blots them out of His memory.

THE TENSION RESOLVED

At this point in our study of God's view of sin, we seem to have two incompatible truths. On the one hand, we see that God views our sin far more seriously than we do. We talk about weakness of character or immaturity; God talks about rebellion. We speak of falling before some temptation; God says we have despised His Word and His Person. We feel we have made a mistake; God says we have defied His command.

At the same time, we have seen that God removes our sin an infinite distance from us—as far as the east is from the west. He has put our sins behind His back and hurled them into the sea. He has blotted them out and will remember them no more.

How can we reconcile the seriousness of sin in God's sight with the absoluteness of His forgiveness as expressed in these wonderful Old Testament passages?

The solution is to be found in still another glorious Old Testament chapter, Isaiah 53. The message of that beautiful chapter is best summed up in verse 6, where we find the solution to the tension between the seriousness of our sin and the completeness of God's forgiveness. "We all, like sheep, have gone astray, each of us has turned to his own way; and the LORD has laid on him the iniquity of us all."

Here we see both the seriousness of our sin and the completeness of God's forgiveness. Each of us has turned to his own way. That is the essence of rebellion and defiance. And though we'd like to think that phrase describes only our pre-Christian days, the truth is we often still go our own way. We do what we want to do, think what we want to think, and say what we want to say. And to the extent that we do that, we rebel against God's law, despise His authority, and defy His Word. We need to remember that our so-called "little sins" are just as much rebellion and defiance as the "big" ones because in either case we have disobeyed the Word of a sovereign God. It is not the size of the sin but the majesty of God that makes our sins so grievous in His sight.

But even though our sins are so serious, God has provided a way of forgiveness. He has laid our sin, our defiance, on Jesus. Here is the solution to our dilemma, the resolution of the tension between these two seemingly incompatible truths. This is why God can have such a serious view of our sin and at the same time be so absolute in His forgiveness. He has laid all our rebellion, all our defiance, all our despising of Him, on His own dear Son.

That is why we can never exhaust the forgiveness promised to us in 1 John 1:9. The sacrifice of Jesus was infinite, sufficient to pay for the sins of the world, and certainly sufficient to pay for *all* of your sins and mine.

If the promise of forgiveness and cleansing were in any way dependent on us, we would have long ago exhausted our credit. But Jesus' sacrifice was infinite. Thus, God's forgiveness can be infinite. We can never exhaust the promise that "If we confess our sins, he is faithful and just and will forgive us our sins and purify us from all unrighteousness."

So let's not abuse the promise of 1 John 1:9. Let's not be too casual about the sins we confess. Let's acknowledge that we have rebelled against God and despised His Word. But let us also not despair of being forgiven. We cannot exhaust the limits of God's forgiveness. Let us accept the infinite value of Christ's atonement and believe that God has, in fact, blotted out our transgressions, hurling them into the depths of the sea and remembering them no more.

Jerry Bridges is Vice President for Corporate Affairs of The Navigators. He is the author of The Pursuit of Holiness, The Practice of Godliness, Trusting God, *and* Transforming Grace *(NavPress).*

QUESTIONS FOR MEDITATION

1. In many ways, sin is a very appealing thing. What sins are you especially vulnerable to? How can you step back and begin to see the true nature—the darkness and destructiveness—of these sins?
2. What does it mean to be "dead to sin but alive to God in Christ Jesus" (Romans 6:11)? Don't concentrate just on the theology of these words but also on how to live out this profound truth.
3. Whether you're aware of it or not, you're involved in a spiritual battle with a dark, formidable spiritual enemy. Satan wants desperately to sabotage your faith. What are you prepared to do to defend yourself?

VERSE CARD REFERENCES

1 John 1:8-9, 1 Corinthians 10:13, Romans 6:11-13, Galatians 6:1-2, James 4:7-8, Ephesians 6:10-12

Gen. 4:3-11; 50:19-20; **Lev.** 16:21; **2 Sam.** 12:9-10; **1 Kings** 13:21; **2 Chron.** 12:14; **Job** 34:31-33; **Ps.** 34:12-14; 36:1-4; 50:16-21; 51:1-17; 60:11-12; 103:12; 119:4; **Prov.** 3:7-8; 4:23; 16:18; 17:13; 26:11; 28:13; **Is.** 38:17; 43:25; 53:6; **Jer.** 16:12; 17:1; **Mic.** 7:19; **Mt.** 5:21-22,27-28,38-39; 6:13; 15:16-20; **Mk.** 1:27; **Lk.** 22:31-32; **Jn.** 7:6-7; 8:44; 17:15-18; **Rom.** 1:18-32; 6:11-14; 7:5-6,14-25; 12:9,17-21; 14:16,22-23; 16:19; **1 Cor.** 10:13; 13:6; 14:20; 15:56-57; **2 Cor.** 2:10-11; 5:20-21; 10:3-5; 11:14-15; **Gal.** 5:13-26; 6:1-4,7-8; **Eph.** 4:17-19; 5:8-17; 6:10-18; **1 Thes.** 5:21-22; **2 Thes.** 3:3; **1 Tim.** 5:24-25; **2 Tim.** 2:22-26; 3:13; 4:18; **Heb.** 5:14; 9:26-28; 12:1-4; **James** 1:13-15; 3:13-18; 4:1-4,7-10; 5:16; **1 Pet.** 1:13-16; 2:16-17; 3:8-14; 4:1-2; 5:8-9; **2 Pet.** 1:3-4; 2:1-22; **1 Jn.** 1:7-10; 2:1-2,15-16; 3:8; 4:1-3; **3 Jn.** 11; **Rev.** 12:9-10.

4
GUILT

Forgiving Yourself
Charles Stanley

Many of us understand that God has forgiven us. We may even have forgiven all who have wronged us. But the freedom of forgiveness still eludes us. There is no peace in our hearts. We are unsettled by guilt. Something is not quite right.

This disquietude often comes from an unwillingness to forgive *ourselves* for the wrongs we have committed. We need to make peace with God and with others when wrongdoing occurs. But we must also be willing to forgive ourselves.

Not long ago, a young woman, whom I shall call Patsy, came to see me. She was only sixteen, but she had become sexually involved with an eighteen-year-old when she was thirteen. This had continued for two years, until he moved to another state. Overwhelmed by her sense of guilt, she sought private counseling—only to become emotionally involved with the thirty-year-old counselor on whom she had depended for help.

By the time Patsy came to see me, she was confused and desperate. She had thought about running away from home and had toyed with the idea of suicide. She didn't know what to do or where to turn. She said, "I know that I'm saved, but I'm so full of guilt I don't know what to do. And if, somehow, I don't get an answer, I know I can't keep living."

"Have you asked the Lord Jesus Christ to forgive you?"

"I've asked Him hundreds of times to forgive me."

"Well, has He forgiven you?"

"I feel dirty."

"But, did you ask Him to forgive you?"

"Oh, I've asked Him many times."

"How did He respond?"

"I just feel so dirty inside," she repeated.

Because of her testimony, I believe that Patsy was a Christian. But what she did was so sinful and wicked and vile in her eyes that she could not believe a holy God could forgive her for two years of sexual immorality with one man and almost another year of intimate involvement with another.

Patsy said she just couldn't *feel* God's forgiveness.

Patsy's story is a familiar one. But the happy ending is that *being* forgiven has nothing to do with *feeling* forgiven. Being forgiven has to do with what God did for us.

Lest we think that forgiving ourselves is exclusively a modern dilemma, consider Peter and Paul, who had to face the problem of forgiving themselves—in a very intense fashion.

After Peter denied that he even knew Christ, "the Lord turned and looked at Peter. And Peter remembered" (Luke 22:61, NKJV). How many times did Peter have to deal with a profound sense of guilt before he was able to forgive himself?

Then there was Paul before his conversion. He had been consumed with the task of eradicating Jesus from people's minds. Paul had done everything he could to kill or destroy the Lord's fledgling church. Though our scriptural understanding of forgiveness is found most clearly in the writings of the apostle Paul, no doubt he, too, grappled with his own forgiveness.

Many of us are—or have been—at that place in our lives. We struggle with forgiving ourselves for things we did in the past—even for mistakes that occurred years and years ago.

- Adults who said cruel things as children or who engaged in sin as teenagers look back with shame on their actions.
- Some women who have had abortions experience a gnawing, haunting feeling of remorse deep inside. Even though they've asked God and other people to forgive them, somehow they can't seem to forgive themselves.
- Men and women who divorced their spouses realize they were wrong and cannot let go of their guilt.
- Parents who drove their children away from home can't forgive themselves for ruining their children's lives.

Yet the ability or capacity to forgive ourselves is absolutely essential if we are to find any peace in our lives.

> He has not dealt with us according to our sins,
> Nor punished us according to our iniquities.
> For as the heavens are high above the earth,
> So great is His mercy toward those who fear Him;
> As far as the east is from the west,
> So far has He removed our transgressions from us.
> As a father pities his children,
> So the LORD pities those who fear Him.

For He knows our frame;
He remembers that we are dust.

—Psalm 103:10-14, NKJV

These verses are a beautiful assurance to us that God is a forgiving Father.

CONSEQUENCES OF NOT FORGIVING OURSELVES

The problem is that some of us are not able to forgive ourselves. We look at whatever we've done and think that we are beyond forgiveness. But what we really feel is disappointment in ourselves—a disappointment that confuses measurement of our sin with merit for our forgiveness.

Sin and self-forgiveness tend to assume inverse proportions in our minds—that is, the greater our sin, the lesser our forgiveness. Similarly, the lesser our sin, the greater our forgiveness. Would we, for instance, withhold forgiveness from ourselves for saying unpleasant things about a friend? Pocketing the extra money when a clerk returns the wrong change? Putting someone down and pretending it's all in good fun? Lying about why we're late coming home? Having an abortion? Calling a child stupid or dumb? Injuring or killing a person while driving intoxicated? Committing sexual immorality or adultery?

Although some sins bring greater condemnation or chastisement in the lives of believers, God's viewpoint is that sin is sin. And just as God's viewpoint of sin covers all sins, so does His viewpoint of forgiveness. But when we choose not to forgive ourselves as God does, we can expect to experience the consequences of a self-directed, unforgiving spirit.

Self-punishment

The first consequence of a self-directed, unforgiving spirit is that *we punish ourselves on an ongoing basis.* How do we do that? We replay our sins continually. And as we do, we put ourselves in a tortured state that God never intended.

If, for instance, we wake up in the morning under a load of guilt (*Oh, what I have done? I'm so ashamed. God can never forgive me. If my friends find out . . .*), we have put the burden on ourselves, even though as believers we are already forgiven. We get up, work, play, go to bed, and sleep in a self-imposed bondage, in a prison we ourselves have built.

We spiritually incarcerate ourselves despite the fact that *nowhere* in the Bible does God say He has forgiven us of all our sins "except. . . ." Jesus paid it all. Jesus bore in His body the price for *all* our sins. No exceptions.

Uncertainty

The second consequence of a self-directed, unforgiving spirit is that *we live under a cloud of uncertainty.* If we never forgive ourselves, we can never be confident that God has forgiven us—and we bear the weight of this guilt. We are not quite sure of where we stand with God. We are not quite sure what He may do next, because we feel unworthy of His blessing. And so we pass up the peace that passes all understanding, and we have no contentment.

If we refuse to forgive ourselves—despite the fact that God has *not* dealt with us according to our sins, that God has *not* rewarded us according to our iniquities—we continue to live under that cloud of uncertainty.

Sense of unworthiness

The third consequence of a self-directed, unforgiving spirit is that *we develop a sense of unworthiness.* Because we are guilty, we also feel unworthy.

When we hold ourselves accountable for our sins, we are indulging in a "guilt trip." Satan encourages guilt trips. He may inject these ideas in our thoughts: *Why should God answer my prayer? He's not going to hear what I'm saying. Look what I have done!* Satan keeps getting us to replay in our minds what God says He has forgotten—and we guiltily oblige. And each time we replay the past sin by not forgiving ourselves, we feel unworthy. This sense of unworthiness affects our prayer life, our intimate relationship with God, and our service for Him.

To a great degree, we paralyze our usefulness before God when we allow our guilt to cause us to feebly—and always unsuccessfully—attempt payment for our sins when Jesus already paid the debt two thousand years ago for *all* our sins.

Excessive behavior

The fourth consequence of a self-directed, unforgiving spirit is that *we attempt to overcome our guilt by compulsive behavior and excesses in our lives.*

Whenever we dedicate huge amounts of energy to divert our attention from the real problem (our unwillingness to forgive ourselves), we try to escape from the incessant self-pronouncements of guilt. Some of us invest huge amounts of energy into work—we work harder, faster, longer. But no matter how furiously we work, our guilt cannot be diminished by our frantic pace. Sometimes we take on two, three, or four jobs in the church to prove our dedication. We teach Sunday school, sing in the choir, and visit the shut-ins. What servants of God! And we end up making nervous wrecks of ourselves.

Compulsive behavior of this sort is akin to saying, "God, I want to thank You for Jesus' death on the Cross, but it wasn't enough." So because we do not accept God's forgiveness, we double our efforts. (Do we really think that God wasn't able to do it alone? That He needs *our* help?) And we begin a perpetual, spiritually defeating cycle.

The only real answer to our dilemma is to accept God's forgiveness and to forgive ourselves. When Jesus took our sins upon Himself, it's as if He said, "I have come to liberate you. I have come to set the captives free." If we do not forgive ourselves because of our unworthiness, we miss the point of Jesus' death on the Cross.

False humility

The fifth consequence of a self-directed, unforgiving spirit is that *we develop a false sense of humility* when we feel permanently judged guilty and sentenced by God. We wear only a facade of humility when we declare ourselves so unworthy to serve God. And our "humble face" serves as a mask to keep us from seeing our true face.

Does this sound familiar? We may be complimented, "That was absolutely marvelous!" But then we respond, "I don't deserve your praise. Just give God all the praise and the glory." Sometimes that's a sincere response, but sometimes that's a response motivated by a guilt complex. When we harbor a false sense of humility, it's very difficult to accept a compliment.

Actually, *none* of us is worthy of praise. We are worthy solely because "we are His workmanship, created in Christ Jesus for good works" (Ephesians 2:10, NKJV). It is amazing how a self-directed, unforgiving spirit distorts our viewpoint and perverts our thinking. It makes us harbor and nourish—even covet—our past errors so that we wallow in fake humility. We become focused on ourselves and on our unworthiness.

Believers need to look to the past, thanking God for His grace, to the present for the incredible things God is doing now, and to the future for what He will continue to do.

Self-deprivation

The sixth consequence of a self-directed, unforgiving spirit is that *we deprive ourselves of things God wants us to enjoy.* Self-deprivation is the opposite of compulsive behavior and excesses. We say things like, "Oh, I couldn't buy that for myself. I couldn't go there. I couldn't do that."

Self-deprivation is like an acid that eats away at the truth of Jesus' sacrifice. We do not achieve a state of forgiveness by arbitrarily abstaining from good things in our lives. God does not ask us to deprive ourselves in order to "deserve" forgiveness. Self-deprivation is self-choice, not God's choice. Do we presume to know something about our sin that God does not know? Do we dare think that we have some new information about sin and forgiveness that God does not have? Of course not. If our sovereign, holy, righteous God has seen fit in His omniscience to declare us not guilty and to forgive us our sin, we have no grounds for self-deprivation.

WHY WE CAN'T FORGIVE OURSELVES

Since we know the negative consequences of not forgiving ourselves, what stands in our way? What hinders our acceptance of God's forgiveness for ourselves? Our resistance generally can be traced to one of four general problem areas: (1) belief in performance-based forgiveness; (2) disappointment in self; (3) adjustment and surrender to guilt; and (4) expectation of repeated sin.

Belief in performance-based forgiveness

Performance-based forgiveness is not biblically-based forgiveness. We can't "pay" for God's unlimited forgiveness by working harder or serving more fervently. The Bible says that God accepts us on the basis of what He did, not on the basis of what we try to do. But we tend to rationalize, *I have got to measure up.* Ever since we were children, we have learned that whatever we achieve or receive is as a result of our own actions.

"Mom, can I have a cookie?"

"If you are good."

Our whole lives are based on performance. *If I clean my room, Mom will let me do this. If I take out the trash, Dad will let me do that. If I do well at the tryouts, I may make the team.*

Then, when it comes to the grace of God and the Bible's teachings, what happens? No performance is required. *Hold it*, we may think. *That isn't right.* But it *is* right. God's idea of forgiveness is in a category all by itself.

As believers, we are forgiven children of God, no matter what we do. This does *not* mean, however, that we can do whatever we like and go merrily on our way. It means that as believers we have already been forgiven of our sins—past, present, and future—whether we confess them or not. We don't have to keep asking for forgiveness and keep working to pay for it.

Our difficulty is not one of being unforgiven; it is one of *feeling* unforgiven. We are separated from God by sin, not by lack of forgiveness. Believers are always forgiven. Grace is an unmerited, undeserved, non-negotiable gift from God that comes to us prepaid. It can't be purchased, and it is offered freely to all who receive it. And that's what the grace of God is all about.

Disappointment in self

We sometimes have a difficult time accepting the truth about ourselves. I can remember a time when God had just done a marvelous work in my life. Then I blew it horribly. The Lord had lifted me up, and I fell flat on my face. I still remember the feelings of shame and depression.

I wrestled with God's forgiveness before I was able to accept it. At least

I thought I had accepted it. Because I had sorely disappointed myself, it was difficult for me to forgive myself for not living up to my own expectations.

It is important to realize that we disappoint ourselves, we don't disappoint God. How can we disappoint someone who already knows what we're going to do? Disappointment is the result of unfulfilled expectations, and God doesn't expect anything of us. God knows that we are going to blow it. And that's what the grace of God is all about.

Adjustment and surrender to guilt

Emotionally, we may live so long under guilt and self-condemnation that the very idea of being free is threatening. We feel comfortable with what we know, and what we know is guilt. We adjust to our feelings of guilt and surrender the peace we could enjoy if we forgave ourselves.

Certain people whom I have counseled have great difficulty getting beyond their patterns of guilt. Even after I have clearly outlined what the Bible has to say about their particular problem and they claim to understand, these same people end up praying the same old prayer they pray all the time. And when they finish praying, they haven't dealt with the issue.

If we want to be released from guilt, we must change our thinking. We need a thorough cleansing of our thought processes. No more thinking, *I know what the Bible says about forgiveness, but.* . . . Every time we include a *but*, we put one more bar in our prison of guilt. We need to get rid of the bars; we need to break out of the prison. We don't have to be there. But we have to want to get out.

Expectation of repeated sin

I know God could forgive me. And I know He has forgiven me. I guess the reason I don't forgive myself is that I know I am going to repeat that sin. These are the thoughts that cause us so much trouble.

How many sins did we commit before the Cross? We weren't even in existence two thousand years ago. All *our* sins for which Christ died were in the future, including sins that we commit over and over again. God's forgiveness is all-inclusive, regardless of the nature of our sins or the frequency of our indulgence.

This does *not* mean we escape the consequences of our sins simply because we are forgiven. It means that we are assured forever of forgiveness, that we need not withhold forgiveness from ourselves just because we might sin again. God forgives us every time for every sin, and so must we.

HOW WE CAN FORGIVE OURSELVES

How do we forgive ourselves? Regardless of how long we have been in bondage, we can be free if we follow four biblical steps.

Step 1: Recognize the problem

We must recognize and acknowledge that we have not forgiven ourselves. We must come to grips with the fact that we still hold ourselves in bondage. *Father, I realize I haven't forgiven myself and am in bondage because of it.*

Step 2: Repent of sin

We must repent of that sin for which we cannot forgive ourselves. We must tell God that we realize that our unwillingness to forgive ourselves is not in keeping with His Word. And we must thank Him for His forgiveness as we confess our sin to Him. *I thank You, Father, for forgiving me for holding myself in bondage, for keeping myself from You, and for limiting Your use of me.*

Step 3: Reaffirm trust

We must reaffirm our trust in the testimony of Scripture: "As far as the east is from the west, so far has He removed our transgressions from us" (Psalm 103:12, NKJV). *Father, I reaffirm my trust and my faith in the Word of God.*

Step 4: Confess freedom and choose to receive it

We must confess our freedom and choose to receive it freely. *Lord Jesus, on the basis of Your Word, by an act of my will, in faith, I here and now forgive myself because You have already forgiven me. I accept forgiveness, and I choose from this moment to be freed of all that I have held against myself. Please confirm my freedom to me by the power and presence of Your Holy Spirit.*

If we are willing to follow these simple steps, not only will we be set free, but the healing process will be initiated.

When we choose by an act of the will to accept what God has said as true, then we accept God's acceptance of us. And we can tell Him that we have played back that accusing videotape for the last time. When Satan tries to punch the button again, he will find that he has been short-circuited by Jesus. We are free.

Dr. Charles Stanley is Senior Pastor of the First Baptist Church in Atlanta, Georgia. This article is adapted from his book entitled Forgiveness, *published by Thomas Nelson, Inc., Publishers, and is used by permission.*

QUESTIONS FOR MEDITATION

---

1. Sometimes you feel guilty about things that you really *shouldn't* feel guilty about, because you haven't really done anything wrong. What are some of those guilt feelings in your life?

2. But then sometimes your conscience bothers you because you know you have sinned. Ponder some of those guilt feelings. What does God want you to do about them?
3. What are the basic differences between these two kinds of guilt? How can you learn to distinguish between them?

VERSE CARD REFERENCES

Romans 8:1-2, Psalm 51:9-10, Proverbs 28:13, Psalm 32:1-2, 2 Corinthians 7:10, James 5:16

ADDITIONAL SCRIPTURE REFERENCES

Gen. 2:25; 3:6-13,21-24; **Num.** 15:30-31; **2 Kings** 19:26; **1 Chron.** 21:8-13; **Ezra** 9:15; **Job** 10:15-16; 11:13-16; 33:9-10; **Ps.** 19:13; 32:1-5; 38:4-6; 51:1-17; 69:5-7; 73:23-24; 103:10-14; 109:28-29; 119:5-6; **Prov.** 13:5; 17:15; 18:3; 21:8; 25:9-10; 28:13; **Is.** 1:4; 38:17; 43:18-19; 47:3; 50:7; 54:4-5; **Jer.** 3:1-3,24-25; 13:24-27; 31:19; 51:51; **Ezk.** 39:25-29; **Mic.** 7:18-19; **Mt.** 5:23-24; 6:12-15; 7:1-2; 11:28-30; 18:35; **Mk.** 8:38; **Lk.** 7:47-50; 17:3-4; 22:61; **Jn.** 8:3-11; 9:41; 16:7-11; **Rom.** 2:1-3; 6:16-18; 8:1-2; 9:33; **1 Cor.** 1:26-31; **2 Cor.** 2:5-11; 7:8-13; **Eph.** 2:10; 5:11-14; **Phil.** 1:20; 3:18-21; **Col.** 3:8-10; **2 Thes.** 3:14-15; **Heb.** 10:1-2,19-22; **James** 2:10; 5:16; **1 Pet.** 4:8,16-17; **1 Jn.** 1:8-9; **Rev.** 3:15-18.

5
PERFECTIONISM
Setting the Perfectionist Free
Lois Easley

When you draw a square," Dad said, "the lines don't have to be *perfectly* straight and the corners don't have to be *perfect* right angles." He was trying to help me see that I really didn't have to be so much of a perfectionist—that I could learn to be content with less than one hundred percent precision.

If you are like me, you can see right away that sometimes the lines *do* have to be as straight as a ruler. But, the point was that I tended to think it was most of the time. Not just when I was drawing a square, but about almost everything—especially myself.

Perfectionism can be defined as that personal tendency in many of us to expect perfect or nearly perfect performance from ourselves and others and to let relatively minor "imperfections" make someone or something totally unacceptable to us. This is not to say that all attempts to excel or achieve are perfectionistic. What I'm calling perfectionism is an all-or-nothing mentality that demands *inappropriately* high standards. It often results in long-term procrastination born of a paralyzing fear of failure.

Contentment, conversely, means to be satisfied, accepting, able to be happy with whatever one has. It is among the qualities Scripture urges us to strive for.

And yet the Bible also tells us to pursue the highest or best virtues and ways of thinking, patterning our lives after our Father, who is perfect. As conscientious Christians, many of us have established our perfectionistic tendencies directly from our misshapen development of this line of theology.

We sincerely desire to please our Lord. We understand that He calls us to wholehearted commitment and obedience. We look at our own hearts and behavior and see that we fall short of this many times. We then logically conclude that God must be displeased with us. So we try even harder to please Him, laying even higher expectations on ourselves than we did before, only to set ourselves up for failure.

45

At this rate we can never be content, because in our minds, God is never content with us. We can never live up to what we perceive to be His expectations. Where does this vicious cycle begin?

ROOTS OF PERFECTIONISM

These theological roots of perfectionism plague many people. But we also learn to think and act in perfectionistic ways from a variety of "teachers" in our everyday world.

We discover early in life that people often respond to us based on how well we perform. My dad's praise thrilled me as a young girl. I would work so hard to do something to please him. As children, most of us soon find out that unacceptable behavior results in some kind of pain or emotional discomfort, often in the form of criticism.

Most people who are perfectionistic suffer from a longstanding habit of self-criticism, often an internalized version of parental criticism. Or they may be carrying around a composite legacy of critical attitudes learned from teachers, religious leaders, and other role models whose opinions carry a lot of weight in young, impressionable minds.

Another root of perfectionism is the desire to achieve, to do an excellent job, to create beauty, to bring honor to those we represent. This kind of idealism is noble and good. Parents, teachers, and pastors rightly work to cultivate such desires in people committed to their charge. But those efforts can backfire when we begin to fear what will happen if we don't succeed.

I have often been haunted by the fear that my work would come out less than excellent. Or worse—mediocre! Workaholism went way back. It was a long time before I could accept a report card with any marks lower than A's as "okay." So, part of what made failing so scary was that the definition of "succeeding" was so narrow. Being *the best* was the way I defined doing *my best*.

For me, one major taproot of perfectionism is related to self-esteem. I felt good about myself, valued myself, on the basis of how well I could do things, what my grades were, and how the important people in my life responded to my performance. I, like most perfectionists, equated my work with myself. If my work was bad, then I was bad too. If my work was good, so was I.

Even when I became a Christian and learned that God loves me unconditionally, it was difficult to break the thought patterns that had developed over a lifetime. There can be many sources of this obsession in a person's life, and most of these perfectionistic roots go quite deep. Though I still struggle with perfectionism, I have discovered a few principles that help me to be content.

ROOTS OF CONTENTMENT

One of the first things I had to do (and still have to do—often!) is see that

God accepts me in "the One he loves" (Ephesians 1:6). This acceptance is based on who Jesus is, not on me or my performance. Yes, the Holy Spirit can be grieved when I sin, and what I do matters to God. But, the critical truth here is that God's love for me has never been affected by my attempts—or lack of attempts—to earn it. That means He still loves me when I fail to keep my kitchen floor clean or when I overspend my budget. He still loves me when I fail to be the zealous evangelist I'd like to be. He still loves me when my spiritual disciplines seem to be sadly lacking.

Paul writes in 1 Timothy 6:6 that "godliness with contentment is great gain." The "godliness" is where the ability to be content comes from. If God Himself truly accepts imperfect me, then to be godly includes an acceptance of the imperfect.

Yet, when I think about what God is like—perfect in all ways—I am liable to get back into the cycle of thought and action described above. I'll be no closer to true contentment than before. What do content people have that frees them from self-criticism?

One root of contentment is basic trust in God. As a perfectionist, I am often trusting in my own performance to get me through. This is what causes so much fear of failing—a false belief deep down inside that says, "If I blow it, that's the end. It all depends on me, and there's no way to repair the mistake, no way to recover or adjust." When I think this way, I'm not even allowing for the possibility that God's role is actually more significant than mine and that He can and does bring good out of failures.

On the other hand, if I dare to believe God's promises to empower me and provide specific gifts to accomplish His purposes in and through me, I have a basis for confident action. So then, here are two steps to get out of the strong patterns of perfectionistic fears and frustrations: (1) Put faith in God's faithfulness, *choosing* to believe the truth about Him and rejecting the false idea that you are alone in your struggle. (2) Act—do something specific—on the basis of God's reliability.

WHAT DOES GOD EXPECT?

Another important aspect of exercising this kind of faith is an accurate understanding of God's true expectations. Paul's image of running a race in 1 Corinthians 9:24 and Hebrews 12:1 implies active pursuit of a goal. But exactly what is the goal? What am I aiming for?

One goal we know God has for us is "to be conformed to the likeness of his Son" (Romans 8:29). But notice that God is the active one in this process. *He* is the one who makes me like Jesus.

So what is my part? Paul instructs us to "work out [our] salvation with fear and trembling" (Philippians 2:12). I am to take an active role also. God doesn't do everything for me. This means I have to make decisions, take risks, think, and work as I grow.

God *does* expect a lot. In fact, He expects Jesus' character to be formed in me. But He does not expect *me* to make that happen all by myself. Jesus said His yoke was easy (Matthew 11:30). Notice that a yoke is usually laid across the shoulders of *two* oxen. When I view myself as sharing the load with the Lord Jesus Christ, it becomes much lighter.

When I try to zero in on what God really expects from me, it again comes down to one thing: trusting Him with the outcome of my efforts, "good" or "bad." Sometimes this takes the form of letting go of a project even before it's as perfect as I'd like it to be. It may mean valuing practical considerations more than "quality" (usually defined as something closer to "perfect"). Even if the external measures of my work seem to spell "failure" to the perfectionist critic inside my head, I can still be sure that God will succeed in accomplishing His purposes.

As I choose over and over again to believe that God is faithful, and I dare to take positive actions based on that belief, I can finally learn to be content—without being perfect.

Lois Easley holds a master's degree in communications from Wheaton College. She lives in Winfield, Illinois.

QUESTIONS FOR MEDITATION

1. Job-related perfectionists are sometimes called workaholics, and a certain kind of spiritual perfectionists who try to earn God's favor are called legalists. In what ways have you been unnaturally driven to attain a certain degree of "perfection" in your job or in your faith?
2. A follower of Jesus is at the same time perfect and imperfect. Think about how God has already given you perfection. How can this perfection have a positive affect on the many imperfections in your life?
3. There are certain basic spiritual things we could never accomplish for ourselves, and so God has accomplished them for us. But, on the other hand, God doesn't want us to be totally passive, either. What part does He want us to play in the spiritual perfecting process?

VERSE CARD REFERENCES

Galatians 3:3, Psalm 127:1-2, Ephesians 2:8-9, Ecclesiastes 2:10-11, 2 Corinthians 12:9, Luke 10:40-42

ADDITIONAL SCRIPTURE REFERENCES

Gen. 11:1-9; **Ex.** 18:14-26; **Ps.** 18:30-33; 86:5; 95:7; 119:96; 127:1-2; **Prov.** 29:25; **Eccl.** 2:4-11; 7:20,29; **Is.** 26:3; **Mt.** 5:48; 11:30; 19:16-26; 23:23-28; **Lk.** 10:38-42; **Jn.** 6:29; 8:1-11; **Rom.** 3:20-24; 4:2-3; 8:1,29; **1 Cor.** 9:24; 13:8-11; **2 Cor.** 3:4-6; 7:1; 12:7-10; 13:8-11; **Gal.** 2:6,20-21; 3:3,10-13; 5:1,6,13-14; 6:2-3,14-15; **Eph.** 1:6; 2:8-9; 4:11-16; **Phil.** 1:6; 2:12-13; 3:4-14; **Col.** 1:28-29; **1 Thes.** 2:4; **1 Tim.** 6:6; **Heb.** 2:10-11; 5:7-10; 7:18-19; 10:1-4,14; 11:39-40; 12:1-3,22-24; **James** 1:2-4,17; 3:2; 4:17-18.

6
ANGER

When It's Bad to Be Mad
. . . And When It Isn't
Calvin Miller

Anger is a towering Goliath that most of us never conquer.

With maddening consistency it dodges the little pebbles we load into our slingshot. Of the basic human emotions that color our faith, this purple rage flames so instantly and so hot that it seems we will *never* get it under control.

Anger often does a special kind of damage to believers. All it has to do is make an appearance and we're convinced that we can never be entirely like Jesus—because, of course, He never knew anger. *Or did He?*

Some theologians would teach us, "Never say that Jesus got angry; say only that He experienced 'righteous indignation,' for anger is a sin and Jesus never sinned." But most of us have to concede that if Christ never really got angry, He at least must have gotten a little ticked at the Pharisees now and then.

Of course the classic case study of Jesus and anger is the cleansing of the temple (Mark 11:15-19), where Jesus takes a whip of small cords and drives out the moneychangers. If Jesus wasn't angry, He certainly *appeared* that way to those He flogged and to those whose tables He overturned. Let's go back to it and find out: Was He or wasn't He angry? And if He was, what does it teach us about anger?

This scene is far too intense to be congenial. Jesus did not stroll pleasantly past the tables, giving the offenders loving little taps on the wrist and upending the tables gently with a beneficent and gracious smile. He was not softly humming psalms under His breath as He hurled the furniture around and kicked the bird cages across the floor.

What would you call it? Indignant? Righteously miffed? I prefer to think Jesus was genuinely *angry*.

Consider the implication in Paul's statement about anger in Ephesians 4:26: "In your anger do not sin." Paul seems to indicate that it *is* possible to be angry without sinning.

I, for one, am convinced that Jesus displayed a *sinless anger* when he swooped through the temple on a mission from God. But before we jump on the bandwagon of self-justification, stash our slingshot back in our hip pocket, and let Goliath roam where he will, let's look carefully at the characteristics of this sinless anger that Jesus modeled in the temple cleansing.

SINLESS ANGER IS ALTRUISTIC

The word *altruism* suggests something given or done for others with absolutely no hint of self-interest.

Why does our anger so often embarrass us? Because it grows out of utter self-interest. We are angry because *we* have been wronged and *we* are mad about it. Altruism? Forget it—out the window. Our anger finds voice in the cry, "Hey, wait a minute! *You're* not gonna do *me* that way!"

By contrast, Jesus' anger in Mark 11 remains sinless because He is not mad at something that has been done to Him personally, but at the way the temple squatters have treated His Father. Jesus may really have been angry about three different things (I borrow this insight from *Barclay's Commentary*)—and each one reveals a selfless ground for that anger.

First, Jesus is angry about the exploitation of the pilgrims. These people have made great personal sacrifices to travel long distances to Jerusalem, and have likely arrived in the city with very little cash. Yet when they arrive they are taken advantage of by dishonest temple merchants. How do we know they are cheating the people? Jesus compares them to bandits (Mark 11:17). Jesus is not personally hurt by these professional salespeople, but He is angry that they have extorted financial gain from the poor people who are so devout in their worship.

A second reason for Jesus' anger is that these religious merchants have desecrated His Father's temple. One does not have to read much about Jesus' life to see that He has an unswerving love for His Father. Whenever anyone casts a slur on God, Jesus becomes angry. This must certainly be why His anger burns so often toward the scribes and Pharisees. He openly rebukes their religious pretense (read His excoriating "woes" in Matthew 23:13-36) for their big professions and their little deeds. He is angry with the Pharisees because they have wronged His Father.

A third possible element present in the anger of Christ also reveals an altruistic base. The temple area addressed by Jesus' anger was a series of concentric courts. The Jews worshiped in the innermost temple; the Court of Gentiles was the circle farthest out. Jesus may have been angered that Jewish exclusivism was shutting Gentiles away from their rightful relationship with God, who cried in Isaiah, "Come, all you who are thirsty, come to the waters" (55:1).

We can see, then, that Jesus' anger was *on behalf of others*—in response to the exploitation of pilgrims, the irreverence shown to His Father, the discrimination against Gentiles. His anger was selflessly, not selfishly, grounded; it was altruistic.

But there are other important characteristics of Jesus' anger that clearly distinguish sinless from sinful.

SINLESS ANGER DOES NOT NURSE GRUDGES

Jesus, I believe, was never guilty of holding a grudge, which I call "second-day anger."

Any anger held over to the second day may become seething vengeance. Rehearsed hate is a great demon that will come in and occupy any heart that makes room for it.

Paul admonishes the Ephesians, "Do not let the sun go down while you are still angry" (4:26). This tendency to nurse our anger overnight always builds to a grudge, which eats at the soul and finally rots it with cynicism. Over time, a grudge becomes poisonous bitterness. That is why Hebrews speaks of bitterness as a great evil, a root that springs up into a world of trouble (12:15).

SINLESS ANGER IS DIRECTED

Christ's anger in Mark 11:15-16 was *directed anger*. Jesus did not clear out the temple because He was in a foul mood and the merchants just happened to be handy objects for a venting session. His anger was focused on their behavior, which was in need of rebuke.

Anger without focus is not a rebuke; it's a tantrum. Children often experience this unfocused kind of anger, flailing out with arms and legs, pounding the floor or whatever's handy, screaming at an intolerable pitch.

This kind of anger may help vent feelings, but obviously it is not a mature response to circumstances. Adults have their own variations of tantrums, such as the slugfest I witnessed recently in the middle of an overheated traffic jam—just plain rage.

Tantrum anger indulges an immature response without regard for its source or effects; directed anger focuses on what needs to change.

SINLESS ANGER IS USABLE

If anger is directed rather than unfocused, it's likely to be *usable*. What we behold of Jesus' anger in Mark 11 is most usable. Jesus may not have ushered in lasting reform (there is, after all, no permanent record that indicates the moneychangers didn't go right back to their posts extorting money from pilgrims the next day), but by growing angry he stated the moral position of God on the matter.

Paul's confrontation with Peter (Galatians 2:11) provides an example of directed, usable anger. Paul got mad. He somewhat steamily confessed that he had opposed Peter "to his face, because he was clearly in the wrong." But Paul was not simply blowing off steam at his partner; he was insisting that Gentiles were not second-class Christians after the first-class, circumcised Jewish Christians. His confrontation was focused on an issue with a biblical foundation, and it had a positive effect in an area that needed changing.

Martin Luther did not immediately change the corrupt use of indulgences when he took his stand at Worms, but nobody could say the anger that fueled his crusade was unfocused and useless. Why? Because Luther had established the normative expectation of God for the Reformation itself. His anger was usable, and it effected permanent changes in the church.

SINLESS ANGER IS CONTROLLED

Right after the cleansing of the temple—for the next few days—Jesus taught there without any further mention of the incident. The scene itself does not imply either a loss of control or an unforgotten grudge. As the psychologists might say, there is no "cathexis"—that emotional attachment between ourselves and our mood, the inability to "quit feeling" elated or angry, loving or afraid, etc. Jesus did not have a fixation with His anger. He directed it, He used it, and once it had the desired effect He left it and went on with His teaching ministry.

Sinless anger is never out of control. It does not gratify the sinful desire to nurse personal grievances, to indulge in thoughts of revenge, to vent unrighteous anger in immature displays. King Ahab of Israel pictures out-of-control anger for us. Upon his failure to coax Naboth into selling him a vineyard, "He lay on his bed sulking and refused to eat" (1 Kings 21:4). Tantrum anger, sulking, bitterness—these do not come near to what Jesus was doing in the temple. Jesus was *not* out of control.

We probably can't say that Jesus intended to teach a lesson on anger when He cleaned out the temple, but He did give us a picture in this event of sinless anger. He is our role model for how to be angry without sinning.

When you go up against the Goliath of anger in your life, examine it against the qualifications of sinless anger that Jesus demonstrated: altruistic, free from grudges, directed, usable, in control. When you load your slingshot, aim the stones at the deposits of self-interest, the reserves of bitterness, the replaying tapes of immature responses, the out-of-control appendages.

Then follow Jesus, your role model, in being angry in the right way about the right things. Strive to "take captive every thought to make it obedient to Christ" (2 Corinthians 10:5), and in His grace you will let loose the stone that fells the giant.

Dr. Calvin Miller is a professor at Southwestern Baptist Theological Seminary in Fort Worth, Texas. He is the author of the trilogy The Singer, The Song, *and* The Finale *(InterVarsity, 1979).*

QUESTIONS FOR MEDITATION

1. Who do you find yourself getting angry at most of the time? A certain family member? A close friend? Your boss? Yourself? God? Why do you get so angry?
2. What's the best way for you to handle your anger? What's the best way to handle someone else's anger?
3. What are the primary differences between godly anger and sinful anger?

VERSE CARD REFERENCES

James 1:19-20, Proverbs 29:11, Proverbs 15:1, Romans 12:19, Ephesians 4:26-27, Colossians 3:8-10

ADDITIONAL SCRIPTURE REFERENCES

Gen. 4:4-8; **Lev.** 19:18; **1 Kings** 21:4; **Job** 18:4; 35:12-15; **Ps.** 2:12; 4:4; 27:7-10; 30:4; 37:8; 55:1-5; 103:8-14; 145:8-9; **Prov.** 13:10; 14:17; 15:1,18; 17:14; 19:19; 20:3; 21:14; 22:24-25; 25:23-24; 27:4; 29:8-11,22; 30:32-33; **Eccl.** 7:9; **Is.** 55:1; **Jonah** 4:1-11; **Mt.** 5:21-22,43-45; 23:27-29; **Mk.** 11:15-19; **Jn.** 7:23-24; **Rom.** 12:19; **1 Cor.** 13:4-5; **2 Cor.** 10:5; **Gal.** 2:11; **Eph.** 4:26-27; **Col.** 3:8-10; **1 Tim.** 2:8; **Heb.** 12:15; **James** 1:19-21.

7
DEPRESSION
Caught in a Downward Spiral
Geoff Gorsuch

I rolled in, armed my rockets, and laid down a barrage that ignited the jungle around the heavy Viet Cong gun emplacement that had been mercilessly firing on rescue forces for days. I banked to the left to get a better look at the smoke-obscured target. Satisfied with the first run, I gave the orders that I had given a hundred times before. "You're cleared hot. . . . Hit the smoke!" All we needed were just a few seconds. Just a few seconds more and we could go home. Just one run . . .

The lead aircraft rolled in, his wing man staying high to cover him. As "lead" stabilized the dive to concentrate on his target, what came up at him looked like the spray of a firehose filled with red-hot lead. The rounds glowed in the twilight sky as they sailed past his cockpit, wings, and fuselage at supersonic speed, missing him by just a few yards. He timed his release and a string of five or six bombs disappeared into the dense foliage below.

A second later, the jungle erupted in a red-hot, smoke-filled fireball, as the shock waves of the blast silenced the gun. But while lead began pulling out of his dive, he caught the last rounds the enemy gun had fired just before his bombs hit. He was unable to avoid the dense, dark wall of exploding antiaircraft fire that surrounded him. The deadly shrapnel riddled his plane. A telltale trail of gray-white smoke behind his aircraft immediately impelled me deep into rescue operations and emergency procedures.

"Mayday! Mayday! Olds lead, you've taken a hit! You're on fire!"

There was no answer.

"Two," I said, addressing his wing-man, "you got him in sight?"

"Roger."

"See any chutes?"

"No chutes in sight."

"Olds lead," I said, "it looks bad. . . . You're trailing smoke."

But, there was still no answer. So I shouted, "Lead, you're in trouble. . . . Get out! Bail out! Lead . . . do you read me? Lead . . . lead . . . Olds lead, come in. . . . How copy?"

The silence that followed seemed to push reality into the surrealistic, as time and the war stood still. Once again, I was powerless. Though wanting to do so much more, all I could do was watch in the hope of seeing the parachute that would trigger yet another set of trained responses in me. But there was none.

I called again, "Olds, do you read me? How copy?"

Clearly on fire, the plane continued to climb in a right-hand turn. Then, as though the plane were flying in slow motion, gradually that climbing turn lost its initial impetus and the nose began to sink heavily into the horizon. Again and again I cried out to them, "Bail out! Bail out!" But still no one answered—still no chutes.

Deaf and dumb, the plane a mile off my wing began its macabre spiral into the jungle floor below. Pilots refer to it as "augering in." The term came from the carpenter's tool, which resembles a large corkscrew, used for boring into wood. It became part of the pilot's jargon because the descending spiral pattern of the tool's razor-sharp thread eerily resembles the flight path of a plane caught in a long, slow, gradual spin. Though a spiral gives the appearance of being under control, in reality it's not. For some reason, the vital interpretation of the instruments breaks down, and unless the crew is shocked back into corrective action, that spiral leads to death.

All we had needed was a few seconds. Just a few. But now, as the nose of their crippled plane fell below the horizon, the long, slow descent to death crystallized. Lower, lower, and lower they went until, through my tears, I screamed into the radios for the last time in the desperate hope of waking one of the two pilots, apparently knocked unconscious by those fatal rounds of gunfire. But it was to no avail. There was just silence, smoke, and a spiral whose tightening turns bored through what little altitude was left . . . and they augered in.

THE DEATH SPIRAL

Since that day, I've seen other spirals and, at times, I've been caught in them myself. Though they were of a spiritual nature, they were just as deadly. For the believer, they begin when our eyes leave the instruments—consciences steeped in God's Word—and we unconsciously start to demand from God what He never intended us to have. Or, we begin looking to get out of life what it was never designed by its Creator to deliver. In doing so, we blunder into the faith-killing insistence that God answer up to our world view. Caught in the height of presumption, we insist that the Creator serve the creature. When He doesn't, we "take a hit," and the spiral begins.

Disillusionment

As the spiral progresses, we find ourselves disappointed, stunned, disillusioned. But when we are feeling disillusioned, it's because we've first been under the influence of an illusion that, like a mirage in the desert, vanishes under closer scrutiny. In our insistence, however, we tell ourselves that if we invest more time, effort, money, and energy, our desire is more likely to come to pass. And so man has been sacrificing since the beginning—for his world view. But what of God's eternal agenda?

Disappointment and disillusionment are the first warning signals telling us that our eyes have momentarily strayed from the instruments and our unconscious desires have subtly moved beyond what God has intended for us at the moment. The essence of sin is to overreach, that is, to place expectations on life that are beyond God's parameters.

We face an enemy who wants to keep us from pulling out of the death spiral once it has begun. His primary tactic is to keep us from getting back on the instruments and his primary weapon is accusation. He's known as an accuser who accuses us daily before God and man. Like an enemy gunner, he fires salvos of guilt, incessantly prodding us toward self-criticism. He's an expert at tearing people apart. He makes sure that we see the flaws in our own character, and certainly in the character of others.

In getting our focus off God's love, Satan can twist the sense of Scripture itself in order to seemingly prove that our faith was ill-founded. Where the Bible speaks of love, he will point out how much love we have *not* received. Where Scripture speaks of justice, he will clearly point out the justice we have *not* received. And so on. He will accuse, accuse, and accuse again. Eventually, we begin to agree with him. As we do so, the spiral tightens.

Discouragement

To lose heart or one's courage is the essence of discouragement. And though we all get to that point time and again—particularly when it comes to the people and projects that have meant the most to us—we must recognize that the spiral is now in a more aggravated state. We've fallen deeper into the merciless hands of the accuser. For if we continue to listen to the accusations—all that is wrong, all that is missing, all that is *not* happening the way we would like it to—eventually we will begin to find reasons for feeling that life itself is against us. And so we find ourselves facing life without courage. Alone.

But coming to this conclusion that life is against us, though it seems so clearly to be an irreversible dilemma, does not resolve the problem of what is *not* happening, either in our lives or in the lives of those around us. In our "aloneness," as the frustration and guilt feelings mount, we discover that we are also answerless.

Depression

Feeling alone and estranged from life often leads to depression. When we fail to find an answer or a world view strong enough to deal with the discouragement of this life, the spiral continues. Faced with a growing awareness of all that is missing, or at least appears to be missing, we spin downward into depression.

Depending on how far into it we have gone, we experience either listlessness and a general lack of enthusiasm for life or a pronounced, stoic silence and withdrawal from those we love. Finally, there are the more acute cases when a person is no longer able to function in a normal manner and needs to be hospitalized.

Much of the post-traumatic syndrome, "combat fatigue," that a minority of Vietnam veterans have experienced is an advanced state of depression. Having faced a murderous reality that was too brutal, too discouraging for their youthful idealism, these men need time and loving care to digest what their beings had been assaulted with over there.

If you have ever skirted the edge of depression, as I have, you know that trying to put it all back together and coming to some coherent explanation about the meaning of life, or at least your own life, is a difficult task. Picking up the pieces of life's broken puzzle, even if you still have the energy of youth, is never easy. But time can heal, if we are listening to the right voice. Failure to get the right kind of help, however, will surely lead to the final phase of the spiritual death spiral.

Despair

It is at this point that the accuser demonstrates his greatest genius and subtlety. He offers despair—as a form of hope! That is, the pain of trying to figure it all out is so great that he helps us come to the seemingly logical and rational explanation that we are alone in this pain. So, there is really nothing to figure out! It's all absurd. The pain and suffering have no real meaning, so we should stop looking for it. Ceasing to look for a greater, transcendent truth, according to the accuser, helps us "cope" with present realities. Accepting this bitter truth, he says, frees us up to take care of ourselves. We are no longer naive children looking for God. We're realists. Living in despair saves us from any disappointments in the future. We're free to expect nothing more from life. And, unfortunately, that's what we get: nothing!

In other words, when our pain and disappointment become so ugly and dark that we see no possible way out, we may decide to either end the pain by ending our lives, or determine to go on with life as an accuser ourselves. As we do so, we become more and more closed to the idea of a personal God who cares and, hence, a higher purpose for mankind. And so we move from despair into a kind of cynicism that masquerades as realism. With more time, we may even become evangelists of despair, openly mocking those who are still looking for an ennobling purpose to it all.

THE RELENTLESS ACCUSER

Returning from that mission, I was under the incessant attack of the accuser. Why didn't I foresee the possibility? But, I had! Why didn't I call his run in from a safer direction? But I had! I picked the direction after studying the terrain with binoculars—and dodging some of the same flak to do so. Why didn't I clear him sooner—or later? But, the timing was right! And so my inner dialogue went. And I was losing.

The other days—the happier days, the successful rescues, the days when the guns had been silenced without a loss—paled into the distant background when compared with this day's pain and self-doubt. Could I have done it better? Had my conscience been as sensitive to my professional training as it needed to be at that moment? What about the other moments, the other days? Days when I had to hit a staging area, knowing that it might also very well be a field hospital. Days of trying to save a village that was being overrun, knowing that I couldn't control where every ricocheted bullet went. And in it all, there were always the innocent, the women and children. There were the days when we would make all the right decisions, only to see the hazards of war negate them. What about all that?

The accuser was relentless . . . pitiless . . . merciless. I could almost hear his audible, laughing voice sneering at me, "And you call yourself a Christian?" Like the apostle Paul, I knew what the law and conscience said. Like Paul, I realized that, given the situation, I wouldn't be able to obey the law and the voice of my conscience—without help. Like Paul, I cried out, "Who will rescue me from this body of death?" Where could I go . . . to whom could I go . . . with all this?

In Aleksandr Solzhenitsyn's apocalyptic vision of the future, *From Under the Rubble*, the past stands out as a mirror of what the future might hold if man does not turn back from his self-destructive willfulness. He describes in painful detail the treason, betrayal, and despair that seized his people during those dark days when Stalin ruled with an iron fist. Surrounded by death, destruction, and the deep wounds of great loss, coming out from under the rubble became as much a psychological struggle as it was a profound physical necessity. Why do it? For whom? For what? In essence, his people were paralyzed by the past. They couldn't forget; they couldn't forgive. The wounds were too deep. Despair reigned, and understandably so.

Then, Solzhenitsyn went on to ask the compelling questions: Where could they take such pain, sorrow, and disappointment? Where could they leave it? What event was big enough to give Russia and all of humanity a fresh start after such barbarity? Who was big enough to silence the accuser when so much of what he was saying was true? So much was *not* right with the world! With *life*! Who, finally, could take so many scarred people and lift them out of their inevitable despair?

59

NO CONDEMNATION

There was only one, Solzhenitsyn said, who could lead us to the forgiveness of ourselves, others—and a new life. The Christ! And only one event in history could have so profoundly marked it that, in spite of the accuser, man could still face life with hope. God died to redeem history! The blood of the Lamb overcomes the accuser by taking all the guilt and shame and, from God's perspective, washing it away. And it can do the same from our perspective as well, *if* we will only let it.

Against the backdrop of despair, the need for salvation—even for a religious man like Paul—becomes evident. Caught in the conscious awareness of his inability to obey the law, Paul knew how much he was missing the mark. He knew only too well how devastating the accuser could be. He was aware of what he was not doing that he *should* do, and of what he was doing that he should *not* do. In the hands of the accuser, the law had become a bludgeon that condemned Paul, pushing him to the brink of despair—something I, too, had experienced. But that fateful day, as I read again of Paul's struggle, my heart seized the significance of his victorious cry: the cry of faith. "There is now no condemnation for those who are in Christ Jesus, because through Christ Jesus the law of the Spirit of life set me free from the law of sin and death" (Romans 8:1-2).

At the Cross, God offered man the power to silence the accuser and to pull out of the spiral. A new principle was set in motion by which the moral order of the universe would now be governed. No condemnation! God's ultimate intention was clearly revealed, in spite of what the accuser and his cynical adepts say. God wants a *relationship*! How, then, could we be alone? Ever since the Cross, that relationship is now possible if we will live according to that new life-giving principle that sets us free from the spiral . . . and death.

Geoff Gorsuch served as a U.S. Air Force pilot in Vietnam. He is a Navigator representative in Strasbourg, France. This article is adapted from his book On Eagles' Wings *(NavPress), which is now out of print.*

QUESTIONS FOR MEDITATION

1. Sometimes depression is due to an organic problem, such as a person's irregular brain chemistry. But depression is also caused by a certain emotional response to difficult circumstances in one's life. What kinds of things tend to make you feel depressed? How much of your depression is within your control?

2. When you become discouraged and depressed, what are some of the positive things you can do to work your way through that dark time (for example, call a friend, read Scripture, pray, write in a journal,

help someone in need)?

3. What would you say to someone who was at a desperate point of despair, ready to commit suicide? What reasons would you give that person for not only going on with his or her existence, but for meeting the challenge to live life to the fullest?

VERSE CARD REFERENCES

Psalm 42:5, Lamentations 3:19-23, 2 Corinthians 1:8b-9, Isaiah 43:1b-2, Psalm 34:17-18, 2 Corinthians 4:8-10

ADDITIONAL SCRIPTURE REFERENCES

Job 6:14-17; 15:20-32; **Ps.** 18:28; 30:11-12; 31:7-10; 34:17-18; 38:6-10; 42:5-6; 46:1-3; 55:22; 69:1-3; 73:21-22; 88:13-18; 107:28-30; 130:1-4; 142:5-7; 147:3-4; **Prov.** 14:10,13; 17:22; **Eccl.** 1:2-11,18; 4:1-3; 7:29; 9:3,11-12; **Is.** 41:10; 43:1-3; 50:10; 61:1-3; **Jer.** 17:9; **Lam.** 3:1-33; **Hab.** 3:17-19; **Mt.** 19:25-26; **Jn.** 16:33; **Rom.** 7:14-25; 8:1-2,31-39; **2 Cor.** 1:3-11; 4:8-12; 5:17.

8
SEX

What Dr. Ruth Couldn't Tell You
Stephen A. Hayner

We are sexual beings. There is no other way that we can live in the world other than as sexual beings—as males and females. Our sexuality affects how we see ourselves, how we interact with others, and even how we relate to God. Our emotions, thoughts, physical sensations, affections, longings for relationships, and our ways of treating each other are all affected by the fact that we are either men or women.

Why did God make us like this?

Besides the obvious function of procreation, our sexuality is a clue to God's nature and how He wants us to live with Him and with each other. Sexuality is not principally about sex, but about relationship. Humanity is plural because the triune God must be understood, in some sense, as plural. Sexuality, then, is a major issue, not just because we live in a sexually charged and explicit society, but also because it is a fundamental element in the reason we were created by God in the first place.

But today our Creator's voice, if heard at all, is frequently distorted. And the voices of our culture, of our relationships, and of our own brokenness woo us with such mixed and confusing messages that we often don't know what to believe about ourselves.

THE VOICES FROM OUR CULTURE

Everywhere we look in our culture there are messages and images that play on our natural desires. Sex sells. Sex titillates. Sex grabs our attention. The voices—and images—of our society come through loud and clear. What do these voices say?

One strong message is that sexual fulfillment is the key to being happy. Both boys and girls are considered to be weird if they are still virgins at age eighteen. So it should be no surprise that a vast majority of young men and women have had intercourse before that age. The message is: "You can't possibly be a fulfilled human being if you are not having sex in a way that excites you—and having it often."

A similar message is that sex is purely recreational. According to this perspective, its primary purpose is personal pleasure, and it shouldn't be taken too seriously—unless of course you find yourself tragically deprived. It's just a normal, biological function—a need to be filled—like eating or sleeping. Therefore, it really doesn't matter how often a person engages in sex or in what ways sex is expressed . . . as long as it's enjoyable.

This underscores the distortion that genital sex has no essential connection with the commitment of marriage. In recreational sex, the partners are toys to play with. What we do sexually is not defined by marriage, but rather by how we feel and what we "need." It is generally assumed that couples will sleep together before marriage and that singles will be sexually active. Wouldn't it be unnatural to do otherwise?

Furthermore, the voices say, we all have sexual "rights." A study of 1700 teenagers recently showed that 65 percent of the boys and 37 percent of the girls in seventh to ninth grade said that it is acceptable for a man to force a woman to have sex if they have been dating for more than six months. Date rape is now a huge problem on college campuses. Administrators in major universities estimate that one out of every eight women on their campuses will be the victim of rape or attempted rape this year.

How did we get this way?

THE VOICES OF OUR BROKENNESS

From the time we are born we receive mixed messages about our sexuality. Often these messages come from parents who themselves were very uncomfortable or confused about their own sexuality. Many of us, for example, learned the correct names of our body parts when we were very young— except for those parts between our navels and our knees. What this taught us was that somehow these parts were off limits, mysterious, or dirty.

During adolescence, the great question in the back of every maturing child's mind is, "Am I normal?" In these impressionable years, young people awaken to a wide assortment of natural maturation experiences, and this can include sexual experimentation. Often patterns of sexual behavior are established during this period, resulting in hidden fears and confusion that last a lifetime.

There is a darker side for many children, too. Current statistics indicate that one out of every four children is a victim of sexual abuse, and that one out of ten is a victim of incest. In a recent questionnaire of people who are considered by society to be "successful adults," 33 percent reported that they had been sexually abused or battered as children. In another study, 35 percent of the women surveyed had been sexually abused by age eighteen.

We all live with the voices of our culture, our own experiences, and our brokenness ringing in our ears.

TALKING TO OURSELVES

Christian voices are speaking a different message. Excellent books, radio programs, preachers, and counselors stress biblical values about human sexuality and the place of sex. They rightly place sex and sexuality in a context of relationship and commitment—in marriage. And they join with society's more sober voices who warn about AIDS and other sexually transmitted diseases.

But somehow the message isn't getting through. Many Christians I meet are full of sexual guilt, either about the past or about persistent sexual temptations in the present, or sometimes just for having sexual feelings. Many experience their sexuality as the greatest competition for their loyalty to Christ. They are fragile and vulnerable, afraid of the inner forces that seem so unruly and easily distorted.

THE VOICE OF GOD FROM THE BIBLE

The counterfeit messages we hear about our sexuality compel us to return again and again to God's voice through the pages of the Bible. His Word helps us develop a sensitivity to what He, the Creator of our sexuality, intended for us in this area of life. And we mustn't look only at those verses that describe what we should and shouldn't do. We need to know how our sexuality fits into all of life and what it is for. Otherwise, we will never be able to resist the counterfeit messages from our culture and from our own brokenness.

Genesis 1-3 tells us how God intended life to be and what caused the disharmony. It tells us truths about ourselves that we need to hear over and over, not only because it is truth, but because the voices of our culture cause us to doubt the relevance of God's message.

For too long we have been persuaded to discount God's good gift when He says, "You belong to Me. I created you. I redeemed you. I live in you. And you will only understand the true goodness of My plan for your sexuality when you live out your maleness or your femaleness in relation to Me." So how can we reaffirm the gift of our sexuality?

1. Our bodies and our sexuality were God's idea. Somehow we don't hear what God says about sexuality because we don't believe He really approves of it. Religious people often tend to be silent on the subject, and the siren song of the world system incessantly leads us to dismiss God's involvement in our sexuality. But Genesis tells us that "God saw all that he had made, and it was very good" (1:31). He called our physical existence good! Our bodies are good. The Creator Himself even chose to live in a created human body! He designed our sexual organs and the nerve endings that let us feel pleasure. And He designed our desire to express love physically.

2. God wants us to express our sexuality according to His intentions, without shame. Genesis 2:25 tells about the delight—the openness and intimacy—that Adam and Eve experienced in that perfect garden. "The man and his wife were both naked, and they felt no shame." God, therefore, is the One who knows how the good gift of our sexuality is to be used and expressed.

When we are in Christ, these bodies that were created as good in the first place now become a dwelling place for the Lord of the universe. The apostle Paul was appalled at the thought of giving our bodies to sexual immorality. "Do you not know that your body is a temple of the Holy Spirit, who is in you, whom you have received from God? You are not your own; you were bought at a price. Therefore honor God with your body" (1 Corinthians 6:19-20).

3. Sexuality is an integral part of life. The world says, "You belong to yourself. You can use your body any way you like." We get confused when we try to reconcile that with God's living in our very personhood. A high school student expressed this confusion when she wrote:

> "I am a Christian. I don't believe in premarital sex and I also do not believe that oral sex and 'petting' are harmless. My problem is that I could not answer a question that a guy asked me. He simply wanted to know why I wouldn't let him touch me in those certain places. Of course, it sounds like a simple question, but I've thought and thought and I can't come up with any more reason than 'I don't want you to.' I have very strong morals in this area but now that the question of 'why' confronts me, I'm really confused."

Author Tim Stafford answered this well when he replied, "Because when he touches you in those places, he touches more than skin. He touches a very private part of your soul. When you do, at last, give that part to someone, you don't want fingerprints all over it."

The biblical view is that we are integrated beings—every part of us is connected to every other part. We are physical, emotional, social, mental, sexual, spiritual beings. What we call "personhood" is the sum total of all that we are. When our sexuality is isolated and described by merely physical acts, we are depersonalized. Casual sexual activity hurts our ability to be truly intimate, truly loving, and truly human.

4. God made sex to be part of a permanent, all-embracing relationship. We can't understand that if we deceive ourselves into isolating sex as a mere biological or genital act. Sexuality was first of all designed to deal with our aloneness. What Genesis describes as "not good" before the Fall was that the man was alone. So God created the woman to be his partner. And the man was delighted! Here was a being that was both like him ("This is now bone of my bones and flesh of my flesh"), and yet different. They were created as beings corresponding to one another.

The closing verses of Genesis 2 (which are quoted by both Jesus and Paul) offer a picture of the marriage relationship. It is described as "becoming one flesh." No human relationship is any closer than this. People must leave their parents and must "be united," "cling," "become one flesh" (literally stick together, remain with, be loyally affectionate) to each other in order to experience this special bond. It is a oneness that involves not just the bodies of the man and the woman, but their minds, hearts, and spirits as well. Yet they still remain distinct entities. Paul marvels at the great mystery of God's plan (Ephesians 5:31-33). Sexuality is about partnership and companionship at the deepest levels.

Any understanding of our sexuality that falls outside one of these truths distorts God's plan and ultimately hurts us as persons.

But unfortunately, we don't live in Eden anymore. We live on this side of the Fall where God's wonderful gift of sexuality has been broken and distorted so badly that it is only under the rarest of circumstances that we experience what was intended in the beginning.

THE HEALING WORD
With the voices of the world and our own brokenness screaming in our ears, how can we ever experience God's plan for our sexuality? Listening to God's voice through the pages of Scripture is one essential step. Even more important, however, is coming to Christ daily with our sin, guilt, and temptations. He knows the abuses of the past (both those done to us by others and those we chose for ourselves) and our chaotic rationalizations of the present. We aren't fooling Him with the lies we perpetuate about our sexuality or the excuses we make.

To those who have been wronged—those who feel they have smudged fingerprints all over them—God promises restoration. He restores us first to fellowship with Him as the One who knows us best and loves us no matter what statistics we represent. As we walk with Him now, He deals with our past. That's what the apostle John meant when he wrote that when we confess our sins, God both forgives and restores us to purity (1 John 1:9).

Really? He takes away the dirtiness, the hurt of having been used? He heals the ugly sore on our soul that we've carried since childhood? Yes. That is one more promise of God's Word that we must not discount. When God adopts us into His family, He works at eliminating the shame of our past in ways we can't imagine. He turns the harm we have suffered into good.

He also works to restore shattered human relationships that result from misused sexuality. When we become more whole and secure in Him, God enables us to face both our past and the people from our past who have harmed us, or those people whom we have harmed. Forgiveness goes in all directions.

Restoration to God's plan for men and women takes human form through fidelity. It is little wonder that the sexual ethics of the Bible revolve around building and maintaining faithfulness in a marriage relationship. This is where the unity that God planned in the beginning can be best experienced.

For those who are married, fidelity provides a context where God's grace, forgiveness, and faithfulness can be experienced in open, trusting intimacy. The marriage relationship is where naturally selfish people can learn dependence on the God whose character and intimacy they mirror in their sexuality.

For those who are unmarried, seeing marriage as the appropriate context for full sexual expression can build trust, patience, and discipline, the foundation for true sexual freedom when the time is right. It also preserves unmarried people from deeper pain—emotional brokenness and the heartbreak of counterfeit relationships.

Consecrating our sexuality is a lifelong process, one that takes personal discipline and other people to help us. Confessing our sins or hurts out loud or in a journal is helpful to some people. Others find more accountability by talking about their present temptations or their past anger with someone they trust. Some have found help in the "twelve steps," made famous in Alcoholics Anonymous and adapted to sexual addictions.

Jesus is calling us, through whatever method, to return to the truth of His declarations about our sexuality and our relationships. He is well able to guide us toward sexual healing, whether we are young or old, married or unmarried. What will those who venture with Christ into the area of their sexuality find? In the words of Tim Stafford:

> They will find healing from past wounds.
> They will find forgiveness for past sins.
> They will find an example—a living, present example—of sacrificial, covenantal love.
> They will find a purpose that lifts them above themselves and their narrow preoccupations.
> They will find joy and peace, which radiate from the presence of the Holy Spirit.
> They will find patience to persevere in difficulties.
> They will find strength to control their own impulses.

The confusing voices of society and our own brokenness need not overwhelm us. Even in the area of our sexuality it is possible to hear the clarion voice of God and to experience the restoring touch of His hand.

"To him who is able to keep you from falling and to present you before his glorious presence without fault and with great joy—to the only God our Savior be glory, majesty, power and authority, through Jesus Christ our Lord, before all ages, now and forevermore! Amen" (Jude 24-25).

Dr. Stephen A. Hayner is President of InterVarsity Christian Fellowship. He lives in Madison, Wisconsin.

QUESTIONS FOR MEDITATION

1. Sex is certainly a biological process, and yet there is also something very spiritual about it, something that indicates a profound, lifetime personal commitment. Look up Genesis 2:24, Malachi 2:15, Matthew 19:4-6, 1 Corinthians 6:13-17, and Ephesians 5:25-33, and then meditate on the deeper significance of sexual union.
2. The word *love* is often used in contemporary culture to refer to the act of sex. Why do you think love and lust are so confused in the language and thinking of modern people?
3. When sex reaches the point that it becomes an obsession, something is very wrong. What specific changes do you need to make to help you keep sexual desires in the right perspective in your life?

VERSE CARD REFERENCES

1 Thessalonians 4:3-5, Matthew 5:27-28, 1 Corinthians 6:18-20, Ephesians 5:3, Romans 13:13-14, Hebrews 13:4

ADDITIONAL SCRIPTURE REFERENCES

Gen. 1:27-28,31; 2:23-25; 19:4-13; **Ex.** 19:14-15; 22:19; **Lev.** 18:6-28; **Jud.** 19:22-25; **2 Sam.** 11:2-9,14-15,26-27; **Job** 24:15-17,21; 31:1; **Prov.** 5:3-6,18-21; 6:23-35; 7:4-27; 30:20; **Song of Songs** (whole book); **Jer.** 5:7-9; 13:26-27; **Nah.** 3:3-6; **Mal.** 2:15; **Mt.** 5:27-28,31-32; 15:19-20; 19:4-6; **Mk.** 7:20-23; **Jn.** 8:3-11; **Rom.** 1:21-32; 2:22; 13:12-14; **1 Cor.** 5:1-5,9-11; 6:9-10,13-20; 7:1-6,8-9,25-28; **2 Cor.** 12:21; **Gal.** 5:19-21; **Eph.** 4:18-19; 5:3-5,25-33; **Col.** 3:5-8; **1 Thes.** 4:3-8; **1 Tim.** 1:8-11; 5:1-2; **Heb.** 12:16; 13:4; **1 Pet.** 4:3-6; **2 Pet.** 2:12-14; **1 Jn.** 1:9; 2:15-17; **Jude** 7; **Rev.** 21:8.

9
MONEY

Life, Liberty, and the Pursuit of Just a Little More
Steve Thurman

An old Jack Benny skit illustrates many people's attitudes toward money. Jack is walking along when suddenly an armed robber approaches him and demands, "Your money or your life!" There is a long pause. Finally the robber impatiently asks, "Well?"

"Don't rush me," Benny replies. "I'm thinking about it."

We may laugh at Jack Benny's ludicrous response, but it represents a very real picture of many people's priorities. For some, money has become more important than life itself.

LOVE OF MONEY

The managing editor of *Money* magazine, summing up a study his magazine did, concluded that money has become the number-one obsession of Americans. "Money has become the new sex in this country," he said. *Newsweek* magazine has described Americans as having achieved a new plane of consciousness called "transcendental acquisition."

Madness about money. Fueled by our acquisitive culture, few, if any, escape its grasp. Television promotes it, advertisements convince us that we must have it all, and state lotteries promise us that we can have it all *now*.

And the problem is not just "out there" in the world somewhere. The Bride of Christ herself has focused much of her attention on the things of this world, much to the grief of her Lord. Some of *us* love money. Some of *us* are committed to the almighty dollar. We love it, and we might as well admit it. We love the things it will buy. We love the comfort and the pleasure we think it will bring into our lives.

As hard as it may sound, the judgment is true: More than a few of us have left our first love and are having an affair with the world. What James wrote to some Christians in his day applies to us as well: "You adulterous people, don't you know that friendship with the world is hatred toward God? Anyone who chooses to be a friend of the world becomes an enemy of God" (James 4:4). Hard words, to be sure, but words that make us stop and think—and, if we're honest, make some needed changes.

STRUGGLING WITH MATERIALISM

There are two assumptions I hold as I write this.

First, just about everyone struggles with materialism. What it boils down to is the desire for more. Maybe just a little more, but definitely *more*. We are convinced, deep down where we make our choices, that if we had more, we would be happier and life would be better.

Jesus said, "A man's life does not consist in the abundance of his possessions" (Luke 12:15). But many of us have bought into Satan's lie: "A man's life *does* consist in how much he has and how much he can get." As the bumper sticker says: "The one who dies with the most toys wins." That's what we believe—the more, the better.

Second, I assume that a follower of Jesus doesn't feel at all comfortable with this struggle. Jesus said it is impossible to serve two masters—both God and money (Matthew 6:24). When you are devoted to two very different kingdoms—the Kingdom of God and the kingdom of this world—you probably don't feel too good about it. You don't like the struggle. In your spirit, you know something is wrong.

John Stott has written about this struggle:

> We cannot maintain a good life of extravagance and a good con-
> science simultaneously. One or the other has to be sacrificed.
> Either we keep our conscience and reduce our affluence by giving
> generously and helping those in need, or we keep our affluence
> and smother our conscience. We have to choose between God
> and man.

Now, if I understand Stott correctly, he is *not* saying that we must make ourselves poor and give everything we have away. Instead, he is saying that we have a spiritual obligation to reduce our *affluence* by sharing generously with those in need. To refuse to do this is to "smother our conscience," something the Spirit of God will never allow us to do with any sense of comfort.

NOT POSSESSION BUT OBSESSION

What is materialism? Does the Bible give us an answer so that we might know what to look for? Well, yes and no. The Scriptures do not give us a definition, but they do give us many *pictures* of its substance and character.

A materialist is someone who is *preoccupied* with the things of this world, cares *too much* for the things that can be purchased, spends his days dreaming only of the next acquisition. And he is frustrated if he can't get what he wants when he wants it.

For the materialist, life is a *preoccupation* with jewelry, or landscaping, or remodeling the home, or trips abroad, or nice cars, or a business deal. Life revolves around these things. A materialist is obsessed with the "stuff" of life.

In the midst of it all, where is Jesus?

He is quietly and politely set aside. Like Martha in Luke 10:38-42, the materialist is "distracted" from God and "worried and upset about many things."

Look at the picture Jesus paints of a materialist in Luke 12:16-21:

> "The ground of a certain rich man produced a good crop. He thought to himself, 'What shall I do? I have no place to store my crops.'
>
> "Then he said, 'This is what I'll do. I will tear down my barns and build bigger ones, and there I will store all my grain and my goods. And I'll say to myself, "You have plenty of good things laid up for many years. Take life easy; eat, drink and be merry.'"
>
> "But God said to him, 'You fool! This very night your life will be demanded from you. Then who will get what you have prepared for yourself?'
>
> "This is how it will be with anyone who stores up things for himself but is not rich toward God."

There he is—a man not "rich toward God," a man preoccupied with treasure for himself. The spiritual dimension is set aside, the kingdom of God is given second place to the kingdom of this world. This is the materialist.

It's important to note that materialism is *not* mere possession of material things but *obsession* with them. That's the distinction we must make in our minds.

Furthermore, materialism is not just the disease of the rich. Rich and poor alike can be obsessed with having more and having it now. All of us can be obsessed and preoccupied with *stuff*. Howard Hendricks, the well-known Bible teacher, puts it like this: "Materialism has nothing to do with the amount. It has everything to do with attitude."

In 1 Timothy 6:17 we see the attitude: the obsession, the preoccupation with money and material things. Paul writes, "Command those who are rich in this present world not to be arrogant nor to put their hope in wealth." Notice, he does not say, "Command the rich to get rid of their wealth." He does not say, "Command the rich to feel guilty about being wealthy." Rather, he says, "Command the rich not to put their *hope* in wealth."

That's materialism: putting hope in riches instead of in God (1 Timothy 6:18). If that's where my security lies, I worry about it, fret over it, and protect it—and if anybody gets near it and tries to take any of it away from me, watch out!

WARNING SIGNALS

You may be frustrated by this definition of materialism: a preoccupation with the things of this world. Why? Because there is no *formula* by which to judge when we or someone else has crossed the line into materialism. We want *numbers* or *categories*: "Oh yeah, *he's* materialistic. He just paid over $150,000 for his house." Or, *"She's* not rich toward God. She owns a fur coat!" Or, "Yep, he just crossed the line. He bought a Cadillac."

But it doesn't work that way. That's not in the Scriptures. Materialism is not a number. The New Testament doesn't give us clear-cut formulas or categories. Materialism is an obsession, a passion, a preoccupation with the things of this world. It isn't determined by how much or how little we have. It's a matter of the heart.

If materialism is so subjective, what are some of its "warning signals"? Let me share a few of mine.

One, when I go from *managing* my money to being *anxious* over it, I know I have crossed the line into materialism (Matthew 6:25-34).

Two, when my eyes begin to wander and I begin to compare what others have with what I have, I know I'm on the wrong track. That's when envy is creeping into my life (1 Peter 2:1).

Three, when I begin to lose appreciation for what the Lord has already given me, when I begin to focus on what I *don't have*, then I know I am preoccupied with material things.

And four, when I lose the joy of cheerful giving, when I'm focused on keeping rather than giving, when I'm focused on maintaining or building my little financial empire rather than reducing it for someone else's good, then I know I am caring too much for the material over the spiritual.

These are the warning lights on my spiritual dashboard. When they start flashing, I'd better pull over and check under the hood. My conscience is muddied, my Lord is grieved, and I can feel it in my spirit.

LOVING, LONGING, AND LOSING

In counseling Timothy about the church's support for those in need, Paul warned, "The love of money is a root of all kinds of evil. Some people, eager for money, have wandered from the faith and pierced themselves with many griefs" (1 Timothy 6:10).

The materialist loves money. It is his lifeblood. Without it he is miserable, insecure, even hostile. But that's not all. Materialists not only love money but also long for it. They crave it. They covet it. They want more; they never have enough.

One man put it so well: "Gold is like seawater. The more one drinks of it, the thirstier one becomes." It's never enough. We will never be satisfied with it.

And even that's not all. The materialist not only loves money and longs for it, but also is *lost* because he loves it and longs for it. "People who want to get rich fall into temptation and a trap and into many foolish and harmful desires that plunge men into ruin and destruction" (1 Timothy 6:9). Temptation, foolish desires, ruin, destruction—not a pretty ending for those preoccupied with money.

A few years ago I was sitting in my office in Dallas, and a man wandered in and sat down. He was nervous and embarrassed, shaking a bit. He had come in for one purpose: to sit in my office and cry, and tell me why.

"I'm a Christian," he said. "I love the Lord. I had a beautiful wife who loved the Lord. I had two children. I had a good job and a good income, enough to take care of my family. We were involved in the church.

"But the money was never enough. I chased it and chased it and chased more of it. I traveled when I didn't have to travel. I had to succeed, I had to make more, I had to prove myself. I wanted more *money*.

"It didn't take long before our marriage was kaput. My wife left me. I rarely see my children anymore, and I've got an emptiness inside that I can't even describe."

This is what Paul is talking about: longing for money, chasing it, making wealth your primary goal in life. And what do you get for it? Ruin. Destruction. Misery.

It's interesting to listen to those who have chased money and caught it. John D. Rockefeller said, "I have made millions, but they have brought me no happiness. I would barter them all for the days I sat on an office stool in Cleveland and counted myself rich on $3 a week." W. H. Vanderbilt said, "The care of $200 million is too great a load for any brain or back to bear. It is enough to kill anyone. There is no pleasure in it." John Jacob Astor, who left $5 million when he died, said before his death: "I am the most miserable man on earth." And Andrew Carnegie said, "Millionaires seldom smile." People who want to get rich fall into temptation and a trap and into many foolish and harmful desires that plunge men into ruin and destruction.

But then, we don't want to be millionaires, do we? We just want "a little more."

THE CURE IS CONTENTMENT

We aren't doomed to materialism, though. We can choose another road. Look at 1 Timothy 6:6-8: "But godliness with contentment is great gain. For we brought nothing into the world, and we can take nothing out of it. But if we have food and clothing, we will be content with that." Or, we *should* be content—that is Paul's meaning. We should be content with the *essentials*: food and shelter. The Christian operating out of the flesh loves money and pursues it with a quiet vengeance. The Christian operating under the Spirit of God loves godliness and pursues it with a quiet devotion.

Ponder the words of John Stott:

> Contentment is the secret of inward peace. It remembers the stark truth that we brought nothing into the world and we can take nothing out of it. Life, in fact, is a pilgrimage from one moment of nakedness to another. So we should travel light and live simply. Our enemy is not possessions, but excess. Our battle cry is not "Nothing!" but "Enough!" We've got enough. Simplicity says, if we have food and clothing, we will be content with that.

At least, as Christians, we *should* be.

I confess that I have never been content with just food and clothing. Here's my list: *Good* food. *Nice* clothing. Two cars with low mileage. A comfortable house—a view would be nice. Vacations, and plenty of them. Ski gear—I "need" some new ski boots. That's just the beginning.

But there's a verse in the New Testament that strikes a stake right into my materialistic heart: "If we have food and clothing, we will be content with that." I'm afraid I'm not there yet.

A COMMITMENT TO YOUR LIFESTYLE

Albert Schweitzer was a medical missionary who died in 1965 at the age of ninety. His standard attire was a white pith helmet, white shirt and pants, and a black tie. He wore one particular hat for forty years, and a black tie for twenty.

Told one day that some men owned *dozens* of neckties, Schweitzer remarked, "For one neck?"

I love that! It makes me stop and think. "For *one* neck?" I have twenty-three hanging in my closet, some of which I haven't even worn.

Can we imagine what our homes would be like if we listened to what God is saying to us here? Just think about it for a moment. "Food and clothing"—the essentials of life. If we were content with these, if Jesus were truly enough for us, what do you think relationships in our homes would be like?

There would be a commitment, not to poverty, but to a simpler lifestyle. There would be no bickering and fighting over money. There would be less worry about the "stuff" of life.

One of my children, while we were discussing materialism and contentment, added, "Dad, there would be more time spent with kids in the family."

How true! And there would probably be more love between husband and wife, regardless of the amount of income.

Imagine what it would be like in our homes if we listened to and practiced the Word of God. If we were preoccupied with goodness and simplicity and Jesus instead of with money and the stuff it buys.

AN ETERNAL PERSPECTIVE

It takes time to work through this struggle with money and materialism. It takes time to grow. It took the greatest teacher of all time, Jesus Himself, *years* to instill in His men an eternal perspective on life, over and above a temporal, materialistic perspective. His men struggled with it just as you and I do. And they struggled with it day in and day out.

Just so with us: The process of overcoming materialism will take more than just an overnight prayer, reading all kinds of Christian books, or hearing a good sermon.

In Philippians 4:12-13, Paul wrote something very much to the point: "I know what it is to be in need, and I know what it is to have plenty. I have learned the secret of being content in any and every situation, whether well fed or hungry, whether living in plenty or in want. I can do everything through him who gives me strength."

Did you catch it? Paul *learned* to be content in the circumstances of life, rich or poor. And he learned *how* to do this in relationship with God. We likewise need to learn to be content by taking our struggles with money to the only true God, who alone can give us an eternal, spiritual perspective in this materialistic world.

Steve Thurman is Senior Pastor of Fellowship Bible Church in Colorado Springs, Colorado.

QUESTIONS FOR MEDITATION

1. How much money would you like to have in your bank account? Why? What would you use it for?
2. Paul said, "We brought nothing into the world, and we can take nothing out of it. But if we have food and clothing, we will be content with that" (1 Timothy 6:7-8). Take some time to ponder what you really need in order to be "content." Should you consider any changes in your lifestyle?
3. In the early church there was a sense of community, love, and sharing. Believers spent a lot of their time together and reached out with financial gifts to those in need (Acts 2:44-45, 4:32). What changes could you make to more fully experience this same kind of sharing in your life?

VERSE CARD REFERENCES

Matthew 6:19-21, Deuteronomy 8:17-18a, 1 Timothy 6:9-10, Philippians 4:11b-13, 2 Corinthians 9:6-7, Matthew 6:24

ADDITIONAL SCRIPTURE REFERENCES

Gen. 1:31; **Ex.** 22:25-27; **Lev.** 25:23-24,35-38; **Deut.** 8:17-18; 14:24-27; 15:7-10; 23:19-20; **Prov.** 11:24; 13:7-8,11; 15:16,27; 17:16; 19:17; 21:5,13,20; 22:7,26-27; 23:4-5; **Eccl.** 4:8; 5:8-15,18-20; 6:9; 7:12; **Is.** 55:1-2; **Hag.** 2:8; **Mal.** 3:8-10; **Mt.** 6:1-4,19-21,24-34; 19:21-26,29; 20:13-15; 25:14-30; 26:6-13; 27:3-10; 28:12-15; **Mk.** 6:8-11; 12:41-44; 14:3-11; **Lk.** 3:10-14; 6:35; 7:41-47; 10:38-42; 12:13-21; 14:28-30,33; 16:1-15; 19:12-27; **Jn.** 2:13-16; 12:5; **Acts** 2:42-47; 3:1-8; 4:32-37; 5:1-10; 8:18-23; 9:36; 10:2,31; 16:16-19; 20:35; **Rom.** 13:7-8; **1 Cor.** 4:2; 9:11-18; 16:1-2; **2 Cor.** 8:1-15; 9:6-15; **Phil.** 2:3-4; 4:11-13,19; **Col.** 2:16-23; **1 Tim.** 5:4,8; 6:3-10,17-19; **Heb.** 13:5; **James** 2:5-7; 4:4,13-17; 5:1-6; **1 Pet.** 2:1; 5:2-4; **1 Jn.** 3:17-18; **Rev.** 3:14-20.

10
STRESS

Tyranny of the Urgent
Charles E. Hummel

Have you ever wished for a thirty-hour day? Surely this extra time would relieve the tremendous pressure under which we live. Our lives leave a trail of unfinished tasks. Unanswered letters, unvisited friends, unwritten articles, and unread books haunt quiet moments when we stop to evaluate. We desperately need relief.

But would a thirty-hour day really solve the problem? Wouldn't we soon be just as frustrated as we are now with our twenty-four allotment? A mother's work is never finished, and neither is that of any student, teacher, minister, or anyone else we know. Nor will the passage of time help us catch up. Children grow in number and age to require more of our time. Greater experience in profession and church brings more exacting assignments. So we find ourselves working more and enjoying it less.

JUMBLED PRIORITIES

When we stop to evaluate, we realize that our dilemma goes deeper than shortage of time; it is basically the problem of priorities. Hard work does not hurt us. We all know what it is to go full speed for long hours, totally involved in an important task. The resulting weariness is matched by a sense of achievement and joy. Not hard work, but doubt and misgiving produce anxiety as we review a month or year and become oppressed by the pile of unfinished tasks. We sense uneasily that we may have failed to do the important. The winds of other people's demands have driven us onto a reef of frustration. We confess, quite apart from our sins, "We have left undone those things which we ought to have done; and we have done those things which we ought not to have done."

Several years ago an experienced cotton mill manager said to me, "Your greatest danger is letting the urgent things crowd out the important." He didn't realize how hard his maxim hit. It often returns to haunt and rebuke me by raising the critical problem of priorities.

We live in constant tension between the urgent and the important. The problem is that the important task seldom must be done today or even this week. Extra hours of prayer and Bible study, a visit with that nonChristian friend, careful study of an important book: These projects can wait. But the urgent tasks call for instant action—endless demands pressure every hour and day.

A man's home is no longer his castle; it is no longer a place away from urgent tasks, because the telephone breaches the walls with imperious demands. The momentary appeal of these tasks seems irresistible and important, and they devour our energy. But in the light of time's perspective their deceptive prominence fades; with a sense of loss we recall the important task pushed aside. We realize we've become slaves to the tyranny of the urgent.

CAN YOU ESCAPE?

Is there any escape from this pattern of living? The answer lies in the life of our Lord. On the night before He died, Jesus made an astonishing claim. In the great prayer of John 17 He said to His Father, "I have finished the work which thou gavest me to do" (17:4, KJV).

How could Jesus use the word finished? His three-year ministry seemed all too short. A prostitute at Simon's banquet had found forgiveness and a new life, but many others still walked the street without forgiveness and a new life. For every ten withered muscles that had flexed into health, a hundred remained impotent. Yet on that last night, with many useful tasks undone and urgent human needs unmet, the Lord had peace; He knew He had finished God's work.

The Gospel records show that Jesus worked hard. After describing a busy day, Mark writes, "That evening, at sundown, they brought to him all who were sick or possessed with demons. And the whole city was gathered together about the door. And he healed many who were sick with various diseases, and cast out many demons" (1:32-34, RSV).

On another occasion the demand of the ill and maimed caused Him to miss supper and to work so late that His disciples thought He was beside Himself (Mark 3:21). One day after a strenuous teaching session, Jesus and His disciples went out in a boat. Even a storm didn't awaken Him (Mark 4:37-38). What a picture of exhaustion.

Yet His life was never feverish; He had time for people. He could spend hours talking to one person, such as the Samaritan woman at the well. His life showed a wonderful balance, a sense of timing. When His brothers wanted Him to go to Judea, He replied, "My time has not yet come" (John 7:6, RSV). Jesus did not ruin His gifts by haste. In *The Discipline and Culture of the Spiritual Life*, A. E. Whiteham observes, "Here in this Man is adequate purpose . . . inward rest, that gives an air of leisure to His crowded life: above all there is in this Man a secret and a power of dealing with the waste-products of life, the waste of pain, disappointment, enmity, death—turning to divine uses the abuses of man, transforming arid places of pain to fruitfulness, triumphing at last in death, and making a short life of thirty years or so, abruptly cut off, to be a 'finished' life. We cannot admire the poise and beauty of this human life, and then ignore the things that made it."

WAIT FOR INSTRUCTIONS

What was the secret of Jesus' work? We find a clue following Mark's account of Jesus' busy day. Mark observes that "in the morning, a great while before day, he rose and went out to a lonely place, and there he prayed" (Mark 1:35, RSV). Here is the secret of Jesus' life and work for God: He prayerfully waited for His Father's instructions and for the strength to follow them. Jesus had no divinely-drawn blueprint; He discerned the Father's will day by day in a life of prayer. By this means He warded off the urgent and accomplished the important.

Lazarus's death illustrates this principle. What could have been more important than the urgent message from Mary and Martha: "Lord, he whom you love is ill" (John 11:3, RSV)? John records the Lord's response in these paradoxical words: "Now Jesus loved Martha and her sister and Lazarus. So when he heard that he was ill, he stayed two days longer in the place where he was" (verses 5-6, RSV). What was the "urgent" need? Obviously to prevent the death of this beloved brother. But the important thing from God's point of view was to raise Lazarus from the dead. So Lazarus was allowed to die. Later Jesus revived him as a sign of His magnificent claim, "I am the resurrection and the life; he who believes in me, though he die, yet shall he live" (verse 25, RSV).

We may wonder why our Lord's ministry was so short, why it could not have lasted another five or ten years, why so many wretched sufferers were left in their misery. Scripture gives no answer to these questions, and we leave them in the mystery of God's purposes. But we do know that Jesus' prayerful waiting for God's instructions freed Him from the tyranny of the urgent. It gave Him a sense of direction, set a steady pace, and enabled Him to do every task God assigned. And on the last night He could say, "I have finished the work which thou gavest me to do" (John 17:4, KJV).

DEPENDENCE MAKES YOU FREE

Freedom from the tyranny of the urgent is found in the example and promise of our Lord. At the end of a vigorous debate with the Pharisees in Jerusalem, Jesus said to those who believed in Him, "If you continue in my word, you are truly my disciples, and you will know the truth, and the truth will make you free. . . . Truly, truly, I say to you, every one who commits sin is a slave to sin. . . . So if the Son makes you free, you will be free indeed" (John 8:31-36, RSV).

Many of us have experienced Christ's deliverance from the penalty of sin. Are we letting Him free us from the tyranny of the urgent? He points the way: "If you continue in my word." This is the way to freedom. Through prayerful meditation on God's Word we gain His perspective.

P. T. Forsyth once said, "The worst sin is prayerlessness." We usually think of murder, adultery, or theft as among the worst. But the root of all sin is self-sufficiency—independence from God. When we fail to wait prayerfully for God's guidance and strength we are saying, with our actions if not our lips, that we do not need Him. How much of our service is characterized by "going it alone"?

The opposite of such independence is prayer in which we acknowledge our need of God's instruction and supply. Concerning a dependent relationship with God, Donald Baillie says, "Jesus lived His life in complete dependence upon God, as we all ought to live our lives. But such dependence does not destroy human personality. Man is never so truly and fully personal as when he is living in complete dependence upon God. This is how personality comes into its own. This is humanity at its most personal." Prayerful waiting on God is indispensable to effective service. Like the timeout in a football game, it enables us to catch our breath and fix new strategy. As we wait for directions, the Lord frees us from the tyranny of the urgent. He shows us the truth about Himself, ourselves, and our tasks. He impresses on our minds the assignments He wants us to undertake. The need itself is not the call; the call must come from the God who knows our limitations. "The LORD pities those who fear him. For he knows our frame; he remembers that we are dust" (Psalm 103:13-14, RSV). It is not God who loads us down until we bend or crack with an ulcer, nervous breakdown, heart attack, or stroke. These come from our inner compulsions, coupled with the pressure of circumstances.

EVALUATE

The modern businessman recognizes this principle of taking time out for evaluation. One president of DuPont said, "One minute spent in planning saves three or four minutes in execution." Many salesmen have revolutionized their business and multiplied their profits by setting aside Friday afternoon to plan carefully the major activities for the coming week. If an executive is too busy to stop and plan, he may find himself replaced by another man or woman who takes time to plan. If the Christian is too busy to stop, take spiritual inventory, and receive his assignments from God, he becomes a slave to the tyranny of the urgent. He may work day and night to achieve much that seems significant to himself and others, but he will not finish the work God has for him to do.

A quiet time of meditation and prayer at the start of the day refocuses our relationship with God. Recommit yourself to His will as you think of the hours that follow. In these unhurried moments list in order of priority the tasks to be done, taking into account commitments already made. A competent general always draws up his battle plan before he engages the enemy; he does not postpone basic decisions until the firing starts. But he is also prepared to change his plans if an emergency demands it. So try to implement the plans you have made before the day's battle against the clock begins. But be open to any emergency interruption or unexpected person who may call.

You may also find it necessary to resist the temptation to accept an engagement when the invitation first comes over the telephone. No matter how clear the calendar may look at the moment, ask for a day or two to pray for guidance before committing yourself. Surprisingly, the engagement often appears less imperative after the pleading voice has become silent. If you can withstand the urgency of the initial moment, you will be in a better position to weigh the cost and discern whether the task is God's will for you.

In addition to your daily quiet time, set aside one hour a week for spiritual inventory. Write an evaluation of the past, record anything God may be teaching you, and plan objectives for the future. Also try to reserve most of one day each month for a similar inventory of longer range. Often you will fail. Ironically, the busier you get, the more you need this time of inventory but the less you seem to be able to take it. You become like the fanatic, who, when unsure of his direction, doubles his speed. And frenetic service for God can become an escape from God. But when you prayerfully take inventory and plan your days, it provides fresh perspective on your work.

CONTINUE THE EFFORT

Over the years the greatest continuing struggle in the Christian life is the effort to make adequate time for daily waiting on God, weekly inventory, and monthly planning. Since this time for receiving marching orders is so important, Satan will do everything he can to squeeze it out. Yet we know from experience that only by this means can we escape the tyranny of the urgent. This is how Jesus succeeded. He did not finish all the urgent tasks in Palestine or all the things He would have liked to do, but He did finish the work God gave Him to do. The only alternative to frustration is to be sure that we are doing what God wants. Nothing substitutes for knowing that this day, this hour, in this place, we are doing the will of the Father. Then and only then can we think of all the other unfinished tasks with equanimity and leave them with God.

Some time ago Simba bullets killed a young man, Dr. Paul Carlson. In the providence of God his life's work was finished. Most of us will live longer and die more quietly, but when the end comes, what could give us greater joy than being sure that we have finished the work God gave us to do? The grace of our Lord Jesus Christ makes this fulfillment possible. He has promised deliverance from sin and the power to serve God in the tasks of His choice. The way is clear. If we continue in the Word of our Lord, we are truly His disciples. And He will free us from the tyranny of the urgent and free us to do the important, which is the will of God.

Charles E. Hummel is the author of The Galileo Connection *(InterVarsity Press).*

QUESTIONS FOR MEDITATION

1. Are you stressed out? Then you're probably trying to do more things than you can realistically handle. Stop. Give serious thought to rearranging your daily routine so that you're not overwhelmed. You may want to ask a mature friend to help you put together a new schedule.
2. There is a real "tyranny of the urgent" in all of our lives. The most important things get pushed out by things that are shouting at us right at the moment. Take time to set priorities on the most important things in your life. Then set up a schedule that will allow you to give time to what you really care most about (God, family, friends, a creative project, etc.).
3. There may be certain stress factors in your life that you just can't get away from. God wants to lift a major portion of that burden from you, but exactly how does He do that (Matthew 11:28-30, 2 Corinthians 4:16-18, Philippians 4:6-9, 1 Peter 5:6-7)?

VERSE CARD REFERENCES

Psalm 118:5-6, Matthew 11:28-30, Psalm 73:26, Philippians 4:6-7, 2 Corinthians 4:16-18, 1 Peter 5:6-7

ADDITIONAL SCRIPTURE REFERENCES

Gen. 35:3; **Ex.** 18:17-18; **Deut.** 28:64-67; **Job** 4:4-6; 7:1; **Ps.** 6:2; 27:1-3; 31:7-10; 43:2-4; 56:8; 73:26; 94:17-19; 118:5-6; 127:1-2; 139:23-24; **Prov.** 12:25; **Eccl.** 1:8,18; 2:22-23; 4:9-10; 7:29; 11:9-10; **Lam.** 3:12-13; **Mt.** 5:11-12; 6:25-34; 11:28-30; **Mk.** 1:32-35; 4:37-38; **Lk.** 21:34; **Jn.** 16:33; 17:4; **2 Cor.** 1:3-11; 4:7-18; 8:13; 11:23-30; **Eph.** 3:12-13; **Phil.** 2:6-7,25-30; 4:6-9; **1 Tim.** 4:8; **1 Pet.** 5:6-7.

11
SUFFERING

Why Can't There Be an Easier Way?
Joni Eareckson Tada

"**J**oni, I don't . . . see why God . . . is putting me through . . . all this suffering. . . . Why doesn't He just . . . take me home . . . now?"

Twenty-one years old, Lori was severely paralyzed in an accident two-and-a-half years ago. Since then she has gone from one hospital to another. The doctors have done all they can. Now they are deliberating where to send her next. Her parents can't take her in. Independent living centers are overcrowded and have long waiting lists.

I leaned my head against the receiver and wondered, for the thousandth time, what to say. Over the phone, I could hear Lori's respirator puffing and wheezing as she labored to speak between breaths.

"I'm a Christian," Lori continued, interrupting my thoughts. "Why do I . . . have to go through all . . . this?"

That's a question I've asked myself many times: Why the battle?

If God loves us so much that He will "graciously give us all things" (Romans 8:32), then why doesn't He give us the crown of salvation now? Is the cross so necessary? How can God enjoy seeing us struggle against an ensnaring world, a corrupt flesh, a fiendishly busy devil? Why doesn't He instantaneously make us holy, bypassing sanctification with all its rugged demands?

Such questions suddenly lose their academic coldness in light of struggles like Lori's. This young, respirator-dependent quadriplegic has been thrust into a no man's land, way out front of the trenches where most of us do battle.

"Be holy," God says to her, "because I am holy" (1 Peter 1:16)!

What?! Is He mocking her? Look. She strives against odds way beyond what most people face! She can't move. She can't feed herself, bathe herself, hold a book up for herself. Why, she can't even *breathe* for herself! Bitterness and resentment lurk inside her like independent personalities patiently, persistently, unendingly testing her mettle. "Why did God do this to you?" they taunt day after day. "Why did God do this to you? And then He commands you to be holy! You don't really think He loves you?"

PEACE AND WARFARE

Every day, you and I go into battle against the world, the flesh, and the devil. The fight is perpetual; there is no truce.

One day we feel like we're in a mild skirmish—playing mind games, reaching for the arms of strangers in our daydreams. Another day we know we're in the thick of a devastating battle—stepping out of our daydreams and grappling with a very real someone.

In the thick of the battle, our enemies can slice through a heart swollen with pride, a heart that runs mental movies of past successes. Or we might feel miles from the front lines, indifferent and uncaring because our hearts are dulled and deflated by dryness.

But if we stand our ground in battle, we have every reason to hope. The child of God is known not only by his inward peace but also by his inward warfare. A tough battle is good evidence of the purifying work of the Spirit in our lives.

The Lord Jesus said, "Peace I leave with you; my peace I give you" (John 14:27). Yet the apostle Paul wrote in Romans 7:21-23, "So I find this law at work: When I want to do good, evil is right there with me. For in my inner being I delight in God's law; but I see another law at work in the members of my body, waging war against the law of my mind and making me a prisoner of the law of sin at work within my members."

These two passages, like no others, epitomize the tension inherent in our salvation: We have one foot on earth and the other in heaven. We swallow the dirt and grime of humanity, yet "have tasted . . . the powers of the coming age" (Hebrews 6:5). We are truly saved, yet still hope for the fulfillment of the promise on which the Holy Spirit is the down payment (2 Corinthians 1:21-22). No doubt about it—life for a believer is battle.

Wouldn't it be easier if, right now, God yanked our one foot out of the mud and firmly planted it alongside our other foot in heaven? The justification-sanctification-glorification scenario would be less messy if the middle part could be dropped, wouldn't it? Why does God leave Lori—for that matter, all of us—on earth to face the battleground of practical holiness? What does God have in mind?

PLEASING GOD

First, when we hang in there, remaining faithful and doing good, our obedience deeply moves and pleases the God of the universe, "for with such sacrifices God is pleased" (Hebrews 13:16).

God is pleased? Is the Lord Jesus, the Captain of our salvation, some kind of ghoul? Does He think, *Ha! Those sinful people are getting their due! Look at them groveling in the dirt of sin and despair! It'll do 'em good!*?

Not at all.

The sign of life

When we struggle with trials and temptations, we should realize that God intends this as a sign of His grace, a spiritual advantage in our lives. Good things are in store for those who strive to be holy. Worldly wars bring out the worst passions in people, but Christian warfare brings out the best—a softened and sensitive conscience, a humble empathy for others who stumble and fall, a fresh love for what God loves. As Paul wrote in Romans 2:10, there will be "glory, honor and peace for everyone who does good."

If you're battling pride, lust, or temptation, you're in a better state than many who have grown numb to the struggle, stagnated in apathy or indifference. The very fact that the devil assaults you, targeting you as a threat, should fill your mind with hope. If being at peace with the world, the flesh, and the devil means being at enmity with God, then being at war with them must mean being at peace with God.

The prelude to glory

God also has in mind that day when He pins on our war medals. Take a look at Romans 8:17: "Now if we are children, then we are heirs—heirs of God and co-heirs with Christ, if indeed we share in his sufferings in order that we may also share in his glory." Those soldiers who face the greatest conflict, yet remain faithful, have the greatest confidence of sharing in Christ's glory.

Margaret Clarkson put it this way: "Perhaps the greatest good that suffering can work for a believer is to increase the capacity of his soul for God. The greater our need, the greater will be our capacity; the greater our capacity, the greater will be our experience of God. Can any price be too much for such eternal good?"

But still the question haunts us: Are Lori's future rewards worth all her struggles, her battle against sin, her struggle to accept what has happened to her?

Yes. For "our present sufferings are not worth comparing with the glory that will be revealed in us" (Romans 8:18). Indeed, "our light and momentary troubles are achieving for us an eternal glory that far outweighs them all" (2 Corinthians 4:17).

If I were a psalmist, I would have to stop and say, "*Selah!*"—"Meditate! Think! Contemplate this thought!"

Our glory in Him will be so . . . so glorious as to more than abundantly outweigh Lori's—or anyone's—struggles. I may not know how this can be, but I know it's true.

THE GLORY OF SACRIFICE

But wait—there's more. God is not only pleased because of our destiny; He is also pleased for the sake of His Son.

Imagine standing with Jesus and His disciples in the temple. Catch a glimpse of the joy on your Lord's face as He delights in the sacrificial act of one poor, striving widow (Mark 12:41-44). Her example reminds us that it is voluntary, yet costly, to remain faithful in battle. And that is what pleases God.

If someone with severe cerebral palsy baked you a birthday cake, it would mean more to you than ten birthday cakes baked by an able-bodied person. Why? Because it would involve greater cost and sacrifice.

In much the same way, our vulnerability to sin makes our striving for holiness all the more pleasing to God. It makes our worship and obedience more precious to Him than they would be if we were immune to sin.

Holiness costs us something; paying that price expresses our willingness to make sacrifices for Him. If He made us instantly holy, bypassing the struggle, what would our faithfulness mean to Him? Little, I suspect.

WE BATTLE FOR OTHERS

At the same time that our striving pleases God, it pricks unbelievers. And that's good! For "God chose the foolish things of the world to shame the wise; God chose the weak things of the world to shame the strong. He chose the lowly things of this world and the despised things—and the things that are not—to nullify the things that are, so that no one may boast before him" (1 Corinthians 1:27-29).

What a sight we believers make with all our stumbling and bumbling! Yet through our weak, lowly, and despised striving, unbelievers are shamed and their boasting is nullified. Yes, unbelievers benefit from our struggles. They are driven—ashamed of their boasting—to God, who delights in unlikely, unlovely people.

If God instantly made us holy, would that not emasculate the ongoing preaching of the gospel? We are *supposed* to "have this treasure in jars of clay to show that this all-surpassing power is from God and not from us" (2 Corinthians 4:7). It's obvious! The power of God to sustain is shown more clearly if appropriated in the lives of tempted and tested people.

There are no shortcuts for us. The gospel *must* be preached by faulty, finite men. It's the slow, painful way. It's the long way—two thousand years long so far! And it's the only way. Peter underscores it for us: "The Lord is not slow in keeping his promise, as some understand slowness. He is patient with you, not wanting anyone to perish, but everyone to come to repentance" (2 Peter 3:9).

ENCOURAGING FELLOW BELIEVERS

Not only unbelievers, but believers also are helped by our striving. My conversation with Lori touched on that.

"Don't forget, my friend," I said to her after an hour on the phone, "if you remain faithful, despite the odds, it helps people like me more than you'll ever know."

"But it's hard . . . to think of others . . . when you're hurting."

"I know," I said, my voice a mere whisper. I had been where she was.

"Listen to this," I said. "Another guy with a disability once said, 'For just as the sufferings of Christ flow over into our lives, so also through Christ our comfort overflows. If we are distressed, it is for your comfort and salvation; if we are comforted, it is for your comfort, which produces in you patient endurance of the same sufferings we suffer'" (2 Corinthians 1:5-6).

There was a long pause on the other end.

"The fact that you hang in there does something for the rest of us Christians. I'm not talking about you being an inspiration. It's more than that. It's a mystery. God somehow strengthens others by your faithfulness."

"But I don't . . . see others anymore. . . . Everyone . . . has gone away. . . . I may help you . . . but nobody else."

A TESTIMONY TO ETERNITY

That plaintive objection, so easy to understand, pointed toward another good reason why God hasn't taken us on the route to instant holiness: We battle not only for the benefit of other people, but also to teach the unseen powers—the rulers and authorities in the heavenly realms—about God!

"You see, Lori," I began to explain, "I had a friend named Denise when I was in the hospital. She lay in bed for eight years, blind and paralyzed. In much worse condition than you. She hung in there, striving to be holy despite the odds."

There was another long silence on the other end and I knew Lori was listening intently.

"Denise died after eight years in that bed. My human logic said, 'God, You should have taken her on the shortcut. What did all her striving accomplish for the handful of nurses and doctors who happened to know her?' But then I read Ephesians 3:10, which says that God uses our lives like a blackboard on which He chalks lessons about His grace and His power to sustain. And He does it *for the benefit of angels and demons* . . . maybe not people, but quadrillions of unseen beings!"

I am relieved that God has not zapped us into automatic holiness. Instead, He has pushed us down the path of practical holiness to reach the unsaved, to build up believers, and to instruct the spirits in the heavenly realm.

LEARNING THROUGH SUFFERING

"Okay, okay," you may say. "So God is pleased with my striving to be holy. So it benefits others. But I still would like to detour around the whole sanctification thing."

Then, once and for all, look at Jesus Himself. Although He was perfectly holy, "He learned obedience from what he suffered" (Hebrews 5:8). How Jesus was perfectly holy and yet "learned obedience" is a mystery to me. But this much is clear: If Christ submitted Himself to such a process, can I, His servant, expect to do less?

Suffering is the path to obedience for us, just as it was, in some mysterious way, for Jesus Himself:

> Even if you should suffer for what is right, you are blessed. "Do not fear what they fear; do not be frightened." But in your hearts set apart Christ as Lord. . . . Therefore, since Christ suffered in his body, arm yourselves also with the same attitude, because he who has suffered in his body is done with sin. As a result, he does not live the rest of his earthly life for evil human desires, but rather for the will of God.
>
> —1 Peter 3:14-15, 4:1-2

NO SHORTCUTS

When I was in the hospital, nurses did their duty properly and well. But there is a vast difference between those nurses and my husband, who now helps me with my daily needs. They acted out of duty; he acts out of affection and love.

We gain no holy ground if we fight merely from a sense of duty or from knowledge of what is right and proper. Love for Christ must energize our warfare. A Christian soldier not only trusts and obeys. He goes further: he loves.

To those who are obedient on the battlefield, God imputes holiness. Some believers may settle for only an occasional skirmish on the front lines, but theirs is a commonplace, almost mediocre, existence. Holy living is rugged and demanding. It is, after all, a soldier's life. But its rewards are precious.

You may never face the same kinds of struggles Lori faces. As I write, she still languishes in a hospital, hoping her name will move quickly up the waiting list for an independent living center. Once there, the striving will go on; only the battle scene will change.

But you will face your struggles, too. If it is true that Lori faces no temptation that is not common to man (1 Corinthians 10:13), then it must also be true that everyone will eventually face some form of severe testing sometime. That being the case, her life should say something to you.

I, for one, don't wish for a shortcut to bypass the battlefield. I am glad that God gives me the chance to fight in the trenches. For when the final battle is over, soldiers like Lori will experience the most joy, the most satisfaction. They will shine most brightly for God's glory. I want to be one of them. Don't you?

Joni Eareckson Tada is founder and director of the Christian Fund for the Disabled (Joni and Friends), and the author of Glorious Intruder *and* Secret Strength *(Multnomah). Joni lives in Woodland Hills, California.*

QUESTIONS FOR MEDITATION

1. What is the most severe form of suffering you have ever experienced? How has it changed your life?
2. Why is it that when we suffer, we can grow in ways that elude us when we are comfortable?
3. No doubt you know many people who are suffering. What practical things can you do to reach out and help them?

VERSE CARD REFERENCES

Romans 5:2b-5, 1 Peter 4:12-13, 1 Peter 1:6b-7, 2 Corinthians 1:3-4, James 1:2-4, James 1:12

ADDITIONAL SCRIPTURE REFERENCES

Gen. 50:19-20; **Job** 1:20-22; 2:9-10; 5:17-18; 13:15; 19:8; 30:26-27; 33:19-26; 36:15,21; **Ps.** 31:7-10; 34:18; 38:6-10; 39:9-10; 42:5-6; 56:8; 69:1-3; 71:20; 119:50,67,71,75; **Prov.** 3:11-12; 20:30; **Eccl.** 7:14; **Is.** 30:19-21; 38:12-16; 43:1-3; 45:7; 50:10; **Jer.** 9:6-7; 15:18-19; **Lam.** 3:1-33; **Mt.** 5:11-12; 11:28; **Mk.** 12:41-43; **Jn.** 14:27; 16:33; **Acts** 14:22; **Rom.** 5:2-5; 8:17-23,26-29,36-39; **1 Cor.** 1:27-29; 10:13; 11:32; **2 Cor.** 1:3-9; 4:7-11,16-18; 6:3-10; 12:7-10; 13:5; **Eph.** 3:10; **Phil.** 1:29; 3:7-12; 4:11-14; **2 Tim.** 2:3,8-13; 3:12-13; **Heb.** 2:10-11,18; 5:7-10; 10:32-36; 11:13-16, 24-27,32-40; 12:1-13; 13:16; **James** 1:2-4,12; **1 Pet.** 1:6-7; 2:19-21; 3:14-18; 4:1-2,12-19; 5:6-10; **2 Pet.** 3:9.

12
LOVE

An Unconditional Devotion
Ted W. Engstrom
with Ron Wilson

On several occasions when my work has taken me to Calcutta, I've noticed a quiet anxiety beginning to build inside me. I know what I'll find. Calcutta is no place for the tender-hearted. A half million homeless people live on the streets. Beggars thrust their dirt-caked hands through the car windows as we are stopped in the heavy traffic. A stomach-turning stench carries across the city, filtering through windows and walls. Stark human misery confronts us at every turn.

In such a setting I have no need to work up a feeling of compassion. I wear it uncomfortably on my sleeve. The coldest heart would break in the face of such suffering. The obvious heartaches and the apparent hopelessness evoke strong emotions and trigger a deep desire to comfort and heal.

Back home, ten thousand miles away, I see that hurting world in my mind's eye, and my resolve to help continues, only slightly abated. But now I must carry out a few more mundane tasks. My car needs attention at the garage. I have a breakfast meeting with an old friend and business colleague. I also have a mountain of material for my overworked secretary, and my son and his family are coming to dinner.

I wonder how aware I am of the needs of *these* people at home. Their concerns don't appear so obvious on the surface. I can't tell what deep longings they have by the car they drive or the way they part their hair. Have I stopped to learn that the mechanic, a new Christian, is getting flak from his friends? Have I been moved to minister to my colleague whose marriage is in trouble? Do I know what bugs my secretary or worries my son?

I want to learn to love these people in a way that enables me to encourage them. I want to help them to cope, to overcome, to grow in the likeness of Jesus. I want to be sensitive to them, not just in the roles that have fallen to them, but as people God loves and for whom He died.

Probably you've met one of those people who always seem to see inside you. They have a way of turning the world toward you and making you feel important or just a little better. I've had such a man in my life now for more than thirty years. He cuts right to the core. In love, he'll tell me when I've made a serious mistake. But I can also count on him to encourage me, lift me up, and gently touch the place that hurts. He practices a healing art, and I want to find the key to this kind of a caring life.

LOVING OTHERS AS YOURSELF

It may sound contradictory at first, but loving others begins with respecting ourselves. In recent years psychologists have written volumes on the need for a healthy self-image. That's probably a good thing. Low self-respect may lead to depression, shyness, excess drinking, drugs, and many other forms of destructive behavior, including the ultimate form: suicide.

A healthy self-image means feeling comfortable with yourself, accepting yourself, knowing who you are. "Having a healthy estimate of yourself" is really a good paraphrase of that part of Romans 12:3 that tells us, "Do not think of yourself more highly than you ought, but rather think of yourself with sober judgment."

When you have a good sense of who you are and accept yourself, it frees you to think about others. You don't have to prove yourself. You don't have to compete and win to reinforce your feelings of self-worth. You don't need to play that old game of one-upmanship. You're free to focus on the person closest to you, to try to bring him or her closer to the Lord.

Actually, God began this process of loving. He loved first. "We love because he first loved us" (1 John 4:19). And if I'm ever inclined to doubt that, I have only to turn to one of the most quoted of all Scripture passages, John 3:16, and see the extent to which the Lord loves me.

The steps toward loving others, then, go like this:

1. God loves me; therefore . . .
2. I respect myself; therefore . . .
3. I can forget about proving my own worth and focus on loving others.

Suddenly, this brings new meaning to the calling to "love your neighbor as yourself" (Leviticus 19:18). In what appears to us now as quaint but pointed language, Jonathan Edwards, the eighteenth-century theologian, called this kind of love for our neighbors "Christian charity," and described it this way:

> Love is not of such a nature as confines the heart to self, but leads it forth to others as well as self, and in like manner as to self. It disposes us to look upon our neighbors as . . . one with ourselves; and not only to consider our own circumstances and interests, but

to consider the wants of our neighbors as our own . . . and to do to them as we would have them do to us.

LOVE ISN'T SELFISH

For many years we used the word "charity" to describe this kind of love. The King James Version uses the word in 1 Corinthians 13: "Though I speak with the tongues of men and of angels, and have not charity, I am become as sounding brass, or a tinkling cymbal." Now I know that our language is alive, and that means it is constantly changing. But I'm sorry to see this word "charity" reduced to use by little more than the Internal Revenue Service. The organization that I lead, World Vision, for example, is classified as a charitable organization. If you send a gift to World Vision, you can deduct the value from your adjusted gross income. You get a tax break because you gave something to charity.

Unfortunately, that's the exact opposite of the meaning the word has held for me. I've always thought of charity as unconditional love, love that "is not self-seeking" (1 Corinthians 13:5), love that doesn't expect anything in return.

That's the type of love I'm talking about developing, only I know it's easier to talk about it than do it. For one thing our motivations are not only extremely complex, but our hearts deceive us. Behavior that we'd like to think is prompted by selfless love may, indeed, be designed to get something for ourselves.

Paul had this in mind when he told the Philippians, "Do nothing out of selfish ambition or vain conceit, but in humility consider others better than yourselves" (Philippians 2:3). The goal of our love should be simply to reach out to someone. The purpose of our caring should be nothing more than seeing something positive happen in that person's life.

This means, of course, that very often we have to put aside our own needs and concentrate on the needs of others. We'll still want someone to meet our needs. After all, we can't completely ignore them. We can't convince ourselves that we don't have what we really have. That's decidedly unhealthy. We can, of course, ask the Lord for someone to meet our needs. Meanwhile, however, we have to make up our minds that to live the caring life, our particular hurts and longings will have to wait a little longer. We must go beyond ourselves in order to truly fulfill ourselves.

OBSTACLES TO LOVE

What is it then that has kept us from acquiring this kind of sensitivity and responding positively to it? In the last few years Christians have certainly become much more sensitive to social issues—nuclear war, race, pollution, abortion, the poor. And it's about time. Rightly or wrongly we had developed a bit of a reputation for building holy stockades and pushing our tracts out through the knotholes. We build gospel blimps, as author Joe Bayly put it, and bombard the secular city with homilies from heaven.

Now, however, we've become adept at organizing, lobbying, propagandizing, and making our collective will known on the grand issues. We've acquired more expertise in mass persuasion than in individual impact. Why? Perhaps because it's easier to carry a placard to city hall than a casserole next door. It's less threatening to urge a faraway tyrant to release his people than to invite a friend to unburden his soul. The former can serve as a convenient excuse to neglect the latter. The truly caring person begins with those he can eyeball and then extends his influence as far as his gifts and resources will allow.

We've also let a number of otherwise good works substitute for taking time to encourage and care for those close by. Check your church bulletin for a list of activities, or check your engagement calendar for a free hour, and you'll see what I mean. Covenant groups, board meetings, church suppers, training classes, missionary conventions, baseball practice, choir rehearsal, clean-up day, ad infinitum! We can recite the creed, chant the anthem, play church, and burn out for Jesus, but never penetrate the protective armor of our friends and neighbors and apply a little balm to their wounds.

CHANGE YOUR THINKING TO CHANGE YOUR ACTIONS

Having said all this, I don't believe that you or I will suddenly turn about-face and practice a kind of loving, caring behavior we haven't practiced before. Turning on the light in itself doesn't get the sleepyhead out of bed. It will take some pushing and prodding and a determined effort to make it happen. We'll have to go after it, develop new habits, build new muscles. We'll have to approach improvement in this matter of caring the way we work on our backswing.

I've found, for example, that the simple act of touching not only conveys a deep dimension of feeling, but it frees me to forget myself and attend to the person beside me. An arm around the shoulder or an extra warm handshake or even an embrace is redemptive both to the one to whom I offer it and to me.

But until about ten years ago, I carefully avoided that kind of contact. Once I learned the benefits and became convinced of the value, I had to practice it. I worked at it purposefully until it happened spontaneously.

In his book *Encouragement—The Key to Caring*, Lawrence Crabb tells how he made some changes in his life, beginning at home: "When the idea first became clear to me that every word I utter should be governed by the motivation of ministry, I struggled to build a new mental tape library. When I arrived home from work every evening, I remained in my car a few minutes and repeated to myself, 'My goal as I walk through the front door is to minister to my family. I sure hope I'm greeted by a happy wife, delightful kids, and a working refrigerator, but no matter what I discover inside, my purpose is to minister in love to my family.'"

The business of playing a tape in the mind is a current favorite of professionals who work in the field of changing behavior. The idea is that an endless loop of thoughts runs constantly in our minds. Like music, the volume is so low we hardly hear it, and like the wallpaper, we pay little attention to it. But still we think—on and on and on.

We can, however, deliberately insert messages that reinforce the kind of behavior we want, such as, "Who are you, really? What makes you run? Where do you hurt? What brings you joy? Do you know the love of Jesus?" When we let this play softly in the recesses of our minds and reverberate in our hearts, we'll begin to respond to the music.

YOU GROW AS YOU SERVE
This single-mindedness, that is, the determination to minister in love to anyone who enters our workaday world, produces an unexpected byproduct. Throughout the New Testament, we find a principle of gain through loss, of life through death. "In seeking the glory of God and the good of your fellow-creatures," Jonathan Edwards put it, "you take the surest way to have God seek your interests, and promote your welfare."

"I tell you the truth," Jesus said, "unless a kernel of wheat falls to the ground and dies, it remains only a single seed. But if it dies, it produces many seeds. The man who loves his life will lose it, while the man who hates his life in this world will keep it for eternal life" (John 12:24-25).

The caring soul can't lose. Make your priority the growth of other people and you'll add a foot to your own spiritual stature. Learn to feel the throb of someone else's heart and your own will beat stronger. Lose your life in the lives of the needy for Jesus' sake and you'll find it. Leave your own self-interests and personal preoccupations behind and see what wonderful things God has in store for you.

For many years I had the privilege of working closely with Dr. Bob Pierce, founder of World Vision. Bob believed that God had called him to remote places in the world, and he literally gave away everything he had as he saw the need around him. I believe Bob would have done the same if God had called him to pastor a church in New York City or grow corn in Iowa. Somehow this man got right to the core of a person's need and then did something about it. The prayer of his life, written in the flyleaf of his dilapidated old Bible, is the prayer for all of us who want to unleash a little love in our own world: "Let my heart be broken with the things that break the heart of God." So be it!

Dr. Ted Engstrom is President Emeritus of World Vision International, a Christian relief organization providing food, clothing, and other aid to the poor around the world and spreading the gospel. Ron Wilson is a freelance editor and writer assisting Dr. Engstrom in some of his writing projects.

QUESTIONS FOR MEDITATION

1. Counselors have found that the most primary emotional need is love, yet they have also discovered that most people are just not having their love needs met. The result is an endless series of personal problems. Is your need for love being fulfilled? Who truly loves you? Whom do you deeply love?
2. Think about God's love in terms of His commitment toward us. What kind of love does He want us to give to Him and to others? (See Matthew 22:37-40.)
3. Paul referred to the importance of love growing "in knowledge and depth of insight" (Philippians 1:9-11). What do you need to do so that your love will grow in knowledge, purity, depth, and maturity?

VERSE CARD REFERENCES

1 Corinthians 13:4-8a, John 13:34-35, 1 John 4:20, Romans 8:38-39, Matthew 22:37-40, 1 Corinthians 13:1-3

ADDITIONAL SCRIPTURE REFERENCES

Gen. 29:31-35; **Lev.** 19:18,34; **Deut.** 6:4-5; 13:3-4; **Jud.** 16:15; **1 Sam.** 18:1-4; 20:16-17; **2 Sam.** 1:26; 19:6; **1 Kings** 3:3; 8:22-23; **2 Chron.** 19:2; **Neh.** 1:4-5; **Ps.** 18:1; 36:10; 40:10; 59:16-17; 63:1-4; 85:10; 86:5,13,15; 92:1-2; 94:17-19; 97:10; 103:1-5,17-18,43; 116:1-2; 119:64; **Prov.** 5:18-21; 9:8; 10:12; 14:22; 15:17; 16:6; 17:9; 19:22; 20:6,28; 21:21; 27:5-6; **Eccl.** 3:8; 9:1,9; **Song of Songs** (whole book); **Is.** 38:17; 54:10; **Jer.** 2:32-33; **Lam.** 3:22-23; **Ezk.** 33:31-32; **Dan.** 9:4; **Hos.** 3:1; 6:4; 10:12; **Zeph.** 3:17; **Mt.** 5:43-48; 7:12; 22:37-40; 24:12-13; **Mk.** 12:32-33; **Lk.** 6:27-36; 7:41-47; **Jn.** 3:16; 12:24-25; 13:34-35; 14:15,21-24; 15:9-14,18-19; 21:15-17; **Rom.** 5:5,8; 8:28,35-39; 12:3,9-16; 13:8-10; **1 Cor.** 2:9; 8:1-3; 13:1-13; 16:14,22; **2 Cor** 2:4,7-8; 12:15; **Gal.** 5:6,13-14; **Eph.** 3:16-19; 4:2,15-16; 5:1-2,25-33; 6:24; **Phil.** 1:9-11; 2:1-4; **Col.** 1:3-5;2:2-3; 3:14,19; **1 Thes.** 3:12; 4:9; 5:8; **2 Thes.** 1:3; 3:5; **1 Tim.** 1:5; **Titus** 2:3-5; **Phlm.** 7-9; **Heb.** 10:24; **James** 1:12; 2:8-10; **1 Pet.** 1:8-9,22-23; 3:8; 4:8; 5:14; **2 Pet.** 1:5-9; **1 Jn.** 2:5-6,15; 3:1,11-18; 4:7-12,16-21; 5:2-4; **2 Jn.** 5-6; **Rev.** 2:4-5; 3:19-20.

Resources for discipleship.

Topical Memory System

If you want to memorize Scripture, but aren't sure what to memorize or how, this is exactly what you need. This package includes memory verse cards in four different Bible versions: KJV, NIV, NASB, and NKJV.
Topical Memory System
(The Navigators) $12

Spiritual Disciplines for the Christian Life

Drawn from the church's rich heritage, this book will guide you through disciplines that can deepen your walk with God including Scripture reading, evangelism, fasting, journaling, and stewardship.
Spiritual Disciplines for the Christian Life
(Donald S. Whitney) $13

The Navigator Bible Studies Handbook

Drawing on more than sixty years of experience from The Navigators, this book teaches specific and time-tested methods of Bible study, giving you the ability to find out for yourself what the Bible says.
The Navigator Bible Studies Handbook
(The Navigators) $8

Get your copies today at your local bookstore, visit our website at www.navpress.com, or call (800) 366-7788 and ask for offer **#2281** or a FREE catalog of NavPress products.

NAVPRESS
BRINGING TRUTH TO LIFE
www.navpress.com

Prices subject to change.